The Month of Mary According to the Spirit of St. Francis de Sales

NIHIL OBSTAT:
Fr. T. A. Smith, O.P.,
Censor deputatus.

IMPRIMATUR:
✠ Henricus Eduardus,
Card. Archep. Westmonast.

Die 14 Martii, 1890

The Month of Mary According to the Spirit of St. Francis de Sales

Thirty-one Considerations with Examples, Prayers, etc.

Don Caspar Gilli

Translated and abridged from
the Italian by a sister of the Institute of Charity

TAN Books
Gastonia, North Carolina

This edition of *The Month of Mary, According to the Spirit of St. Francis de Sales* is from the edition published by Robert Washbourne, London, 1890. It was retypeset and published in 2025 by TAN Books.

Cover design by Caroline Green

Cover image: Madonna and Child by Giovanni Battista Salvi da Sassoferrato. Public domain via Wikimedia Commons.

ISBN: 978-1-5051-3611-1
Kindle ISBN: 978-1-5051-3748-4
ePUB ISBN: 978-1-5051-3747-7

Published in the United States by
TAN Books
PO Box 269
Gastonia, NC 28053
www.TANBooks.com

Printed in the United States of America

Contents

Preface

Of the many who by their writings have laboured to celebrate the sublime prerogatives and virtues of the Mother of God, there is not one whose language is more adapted to the devotions of the month of Mary than St. Francis de Sales. Everything, says a pious author, in this admirable Saint enchants and fascinates us; whoever reads his writings attentively, feels constrained, not only to honour and venerate him, but also to love him. With him there is a peculiar grace to console, as well as to perfect, the soul. He adapts himself to the capacities of humble minds, whilst no one has more knowledge than he of the most exalted perfection.

The sweet mildness of this Saint sprang from the meekness of which his soul was full. It is a difficult task to preserve peace in the soul, and well he knew it, declaring that he 'lived in a continual fear of losing, in one quarter of an hour, all that meekness which he had acquired by twenty years of combat.' St. Bonaventure learnt all his science at the foot of the Crucifix, and it was there, also, that St. Francis acquired all his benignity, fighting for it, we may say, hand-to-hand against his natural impetuosity. This virtue by degrees penetrated the inmost parts of his soul, so that it was not only manifested in all the actions of his life, but it directed also his pen, and enabled him to make use of the most delicate comparisons and ingenious images. All that is sweet, and pure, and amiable in Nature—doves, bees, flowers, all took hold of his imagination. From his lips, as well as from his pen, issued loving invitations to perfection. His singular privilege, however, is that this meekness and grace appear always fresh to the devout reader, and are ever pleasing, even when he lays open the festering wounds of the heart. The great Fénélon, whose spirit and heart so vividly retraced the holy Bishop of Geneva, thus wrote to a lady: 'The books most useful for you are those of St. Francis de Sales. Everything in them is amiable and consoling; everything is solid experience, simple practice, and the feeling and light of grace. *To have become accustomed to this kind of food is a mark of great perfection.*' Bishop Parisis also says: 'Everything that can contribute to make this most amiable of Saints more known to the world, is of the greatest utility to the cause of religion.'

For this reason we have composed this little work. It is a sort of résumé of the doctrine of St. Francis de Sales upon the prerogatives and virtues of the august Queen of Heaven, and we may gather a delicious bouquet for her month of May. Hence the devout reader will always meet with the genuine text of the Saint without any paraphrase, though not always in consecutive order. In each of the thirty-one considerations we have been obliged to discard those matters which did not relate to our subject. However, such suppressions only produce greater clearness in the whole work. We must say two words upon the manner in which this exercise can be rendered fruitful:

1. If you are not able to assist at the public services or devotions in honour of the Blessed Virgin in your own church, erect a little altar to Mary in your house, and adorn her picture, or statue, with flowers, and there, every day, either alone or with others of your household, meditate upon her virtues, and implore her powerful intercession.

2. It will be an excellent preparation to spend the last day of April in holy recollection, and to examine what is the principal passion that you will sacrifice to Mary during the course of the month, and the grace or virtue that you propose to obtain from God by recurring to her intercession. Do not fear to ask too much, she is the Mother of God, and our Mother also.

3. Read every day the appointed meditation, with tranquillity and recollection, that your soul may relish the subject, and apply what is read to its own necessities. After your lecture, follow this advice of St. Francis de Sales: 'When you have concluded your prayer, take a little walk and gather a small nosegay of devotion from the considerations you have made, that you may inhale its spiritual odour throughout the day.'

4. You should consider it a duty to approach the holy Sacraments more frequently than usual during the month, and never leave the Altar of Mary without having made a spiritual communion.

5. Let no day pass, or, at least, no Saturday, without practising some mortification, sanctified and directed by obedience. 'Our devotion, however small,' said St. John Berchmans, 'is always pleasing to Mary, provided it be constant.' But let us not forget that interior mortifications are the most perfect; such as to abstain from speaking or looking about without necessity, etc., because in such mortifications there is less danger of vainglory, and they attack our passions in the innermost depths of the heart.

6. Endeavour also to become familiar with prayers of aspiration to Mary. 'This kind of prayer,' says St. Francis de Sales, 'may supply for every other kind, but no other kind of prayer can supply for this. Spiritual exercises without aspirations are like a firmament without stars, or a tree without leaves.'

7. The month should be concluded by an offering of the heart to Jesus and Mary, after Holy Communion. And that you may more securely persevere in the service of the best of all Mothers, let it be your care to renew your resolutions every Saturday, to examine in what manner you have kept them, and

by a protestation of sorrow for past omissions, and a determination of greater fidelity for the future, to repair the failings of the week.

The sovereign Pontiff Pius VII. has granted to all who shall say some public or private prayers in honour of the most holy Virgin Mary during the course of the month of May, three hundred days Indulgence each day, and a Plenary Indulgence once in the month if, having confessed and Communicated, they pray for the holy Church.

The same sovereign Pontiff has granted to all the faithful who, with a contrite heart, shall recite the Litany of Loreto, three hundred days Indulgence each time. All these Indulgences are applicable to the souls in Purgatory.

Protestation

In conformity with the decree of the sovereign Pontiff Urban VIII., I declare that I wish to give only a purely human authority to all the miraculous facts related in this work, excepting those that are confirmed by the decisions of the Holy, Catholic, Apostolic, and Roman Church, to whose infallible judgment I intend to submit my person and my writings; nor shall I cease to declare myself her respectful son, believing all that she proposes to my belief, because she is the sole depositary here on earth of sound doctrine, of faith, and of catholic unity.

Preliminary Instruction

Doctrine of St. Francis de Sales upon Devotion to Mary

Holy Church, speaking of the most Blessed Virgin, says that she went up from the desert of this world *flowing with delights, leaning upon her Beloved.* In fact, all the praises bestowed upon the Saints, and upon Mary in particular, terminate in Christ our Lord; because all these praises should be directed to the glory of her Divine Son, Who led her by His grace to the most exalted degree of merit and happiness.

It is related in Scripture that the Queen of Saba, taking a multitude of gifts to Jerusalem, offered them *all* to Solomon. It is thus that all the Saints act—and the Mother of God especially. She is ever attentive to recognise that her virtues, her perfections, her merits, and her happiness proceed from the mercy of her Divine Son, Who is alone their source, their origin, and perfection: *Soli Deo honor et gloria*. All honour and glory to God alone; all should return to Him, because *from Him alone is every perfect gift.*

If Mary be holy, who is it that sanctified her but her Divine Son? If she be saved, who was her Saviour but Jesus Christ?—*Innixa super dilectum suum*. Her whole happiness has its foundation in the mercy of her Divine Son. She may be called a lily of purity and innocence. This lily has acquired all its purity by being washed in the Blood of the Immaculate Lamb. She is a rose, on account of the ardour of her love, and her rich vermilion can be nought else than the Blood of her Son. If she is likened to fumes of odoriferous sweetness, the fire which produces them is the charity of her Divine Son and the wood of the Cross; in a word, everywhere and in everything, Mary is leaning upon her Beloved. Behold, devout souls, how we ought to be jealous of the honour of Jesus Christ. Do not imitate the enemies of holy Church, who think that they honour the Son more perfectly by refusing all honour to the Mother. On the contrary, the worship of the Mother is referred to the Son, and thus exalts His glory and mercy all the more.

In order to show more clearly the purity of the worship which holy Church pays to the most Blessed Virgin, I will mention two contrary heresies, both equally injurious to the veneration deservedly due to Our Lady. One of these heresies sinned by excess; calling Mary *the Goddess of Heaven*, and offering sacrifices to her as such; the other sinned by default, condemning all honour paid to Our Lady. The Church, who walks in the royal road of moderation, in which virtue consists, condemned both these heresies, defining against the former that no sacrifice whatever could be offered to Mary, as she was a pure creature; and against the latter, that this holy Virgin, being Mother of God the Son, was worthy of special worship, infinitely less than that of her Son, but incomparably greater than that of all the other Saints. To the first, she says, that the Virgin is simply a creature, yet so holy, so perfect, so closely united to her Son, and so much loved by God, as to render it impossible to love the Son sincerely without loving and honouring the Mother. To the second, she says, sacrifice is the supreme worship of latria, due to the Creator alone, and the Blessed Virgin is simply a creature, although most excellent. Indeed, in speaking of Mary, I call her more the creature of God and of her Son than the rest of creation; because God created greater perfections in her than in all other creatures, and she had a greater share in the Redemption than all others, being rescued not only from sin but from the power and inclination to sin. And who does not know that it is a greater benefit to rescue a person from slavery before he is made a slave, than to deliver him after he has become captive! How far are we then from placing the Son and the Mother on an equality, as our adversaries falsely assert?

It is true that we call her beautiful, and the most beautiful amongst creatures; but she is beautiful *as the moon*, which receives its light from the sun; because all her glory is communicated to her by her Son. Pliny writes that the thorn, named *aspalathum*, is not naturally odoriferous, but that if the rainbow rests upon it, it quickly exhales a rare and sweet odour. The holy Virgin is a thorn of that burning bush which Moses saw and which was not consumed, as the Church says: '*Rubum quem viderat Moyses incombustum, conservatam agnovimus tuam laudabilem virginitatem*'. Of herself alone, she is certainly unworthy of our worship, for she is without odour. But when the great sign of reconciliation between God and men came and rested upon this holy thorn—first, by His grace in her Immaculate Conception, and afterwards at the

Incarnation, when God became her Son, and reposed in her immaculate bosom—then, indeed, so great became the fragrance of this thorn that no other plant ever could produce before God so sweet and pleasing an odour. Nor will He ever reject the prayers that are perfumed in this fragrance. We repeat that all this perfume came to her from her Divine Son.

Jesus Christ is our Advocate, and so is Mary; but with what difference! In right of justice, the Saviour is alone our Advocate, because when He pleads our cause He justifies His petition by showing His Blood and His Cross. He does not hide our debts from His Father; but at the same time He urges the value of the price that He has laid down for our salvation. Mary and all the Saints exercise, also, the office of advocate in our favour; it is only by way of intercession. They entreat the Divine Justice to pardon our iniquities; but it is through the merits of the Passion of Jesus Christ. In a word, they do not add their prayers to the prayers of the Saviour, but to ours; in order to help us to obtain the graces which are necessary for our eternal salvation.

The Eve of the Month of Mary: The Immaculate Conception

The wonderful variety which is observable in the works of nature gives us a very high idea of the immeasurable riches of the Almighty Creator. And yet He manifests His power still more in the supernatural order, and the wonderful diversity of the works of grace preaches more loudly the munificence of His mercy. God, in the excess of His goodness, did not merely grant a general redemption to men, sufficient for the salvation of each one, but He diversified and multiplied the supernatural gifts which accompany this redemption with infinite liberality and wonderful variety. But His highest favours were lavished upon the most holy Virgin. From all eternity the Heavenly Father had ordained in His love to form her heart to the perfection of charity, that she might love His Divine Son with the most perfect maternal love—as He had loved Him from all eternity with the most perfect paternal love. The Son of God cast His eyes upon this Virgin, and chose her for His Mother, and co-operator in the great work of the world's redemption, a merciful Mother, a most powerful advocate of mankind—the most amiable, the most loving, and the most beloved of all creatures.

It is the opinion of many theologians that our Lord sanctified St. John the Baptist in the womb of St. Elizabeth, by a ray of His light and grace, and gave him the use of reason together with the gift of faith, so that he knew his God, hidden in the immaculate womb of Mary, adored Him, and consecrated himself to His service. If such a grace were granted by Our Lord to His precursor, who can doubt for a moment that He should have granted not only a similar, but a much greater privilege to her whom He Himself had chosen for His Mother, and that He should not only have sanctified her in the womb of her mother, St. Anne, but should have, moreover, raised her from the very first instant of her conception to a state of purity and sanctity?

The adorable Redeemer of the human race, the eternal object of the love of His Heavenly Father, considered His Mother from that first moment, as a delicious garden which was to produce the fruit of eternal life, and He cultivated this garden in order that every kind of perfection should flourish therein. He adorned her with the gold of charity and with a wondrous variety of virtues, that she might be able to sit at His side as a Queen—that is to say, occupy the first place amongst the elect, and, in this manner, enjoy the delights that are found at the right hand of the Eternal God.

This Divine Mother was redeemed, therefore, in a manner becoming the dignity of the Son, for Whom she was created. Hence she was preserved from reprobation and from all danger of it, because she was enriched with the perfection of grace and with everything necessary for its preservation. Well is she compared to a beautiful aurora, or dawn, which, from its very beginning, went on increasing until it reached its perfect day. O first-fruit of the Redemption! O masterpiece of the Redeemer! It is just, indeed, O my Divine Saviour, that as a Son full of love and devotion towards Thy Mother, in preventing her with the blessings of Heaven, Thou shouldest have preserved her, not only from sin like the Angels, but even from every danger of sinning, and shouldest, moreover, have removed from her path all that could hinder or even retard her in the exercise of Thy holy love. It was written in Thy eternal decrees that Thou wouldest at one day prefer her to all rational creatures who were dear to Thy Divine Heart, and that Thou wouldest call her *the beloved object of Thy predilection, Thy dove, Thy spotless and beautiful one, perfect beyond compare*.

A special privilege was reserved for Mary, worthy of a Son Who loved her with an infinite love, and Who, being infinitely good, wise and perfect, was to choose for Himself a Mother, and form her according to His own heart. He willed then that the grace of Redemption should be applied to her as a preservative remedy. Like the waters of the Jordan that, in the days of Josue, interrupted their course through respect for the Ark of the Covenant, so the stream of original corruption stayed its course at the feet of Mary, at the conception of this living tabernacle of the Eternal Covenant.

From the first instant of her conception, Mary knew her God, and loved Him sovereignly; from that moment she became impeccable, through the special assistance of the divine protection, and through the continual inflow of efficacious and preventing graces, to which she never offered the slightest resistance. God not only adorned her with the most abundant habitual grace, but He preserved it in her, keeping her always free from every evil inclination, every idle thought, and every feeling in the slightest degree contrary to the most perfect sanctity.

As to her body, we may believe it was endowed with singular perfections. St. Joachim and St. Anne received her from God through a particular, and we may say, even a miraculous grace, so that she was one of the most excellent works of the Holy Ghost, and breathed only sanctity and purity. This Queen loved, then, her virginal body, not only because it was docile, humble, pure and obedient to Divine Love, but still more because from it was formed the Body of her Saviour.

Truly has this holy Virgin been called *elect as the sun*, because as the sun shines resplendent above all the stars, through the excellence of its prerogatives, so there is no one amongst all the Saints who has obtained, or can ever obtain, graces superior to those bestowed upon Mary. There are Saints who have received signal graces from our Lord, and these, compared with the rest of the world, are like queens crowned with charity, and occupy a distinguished position in the love of our Divine Saviour. But His most blessed Mother is the Queen of all Queens, for she is not only crowned with charity, but with the perfection of charity, and to use an expression of the Holy Spirit, Who says that *the Son is the crown of the Father*; her crown is in truth her Son; that is to say, the sovereign object of charity, the Eternal Love, forms her crown.

SPIRITUAL FLOWERS

How lovely is the rose! and yet it causes great sadness in my soul. It reminds me of my sin, on account of which the earth was condemned to produce thorns.—*St. Basil.*

Mary, conceived without sin, is compared to the incorruptible cedar, the scent of which puts serpents to flight.—*St. Alphonsus Liguori.*

How great will be our happiness in heaven, where we shall be able to contemplate Mary, to love her and be loved by her; for she alone forms a paradise of delights. Mary is truly, after God, all that is beautiful, sweet, glorious and amiable in that celestial realm; all is in Mary, all through Mary, all, in fine, is hers.—*St. Bonaventure.*

Nothing is of greater service to our soul, nor more sustains and strengthens it, than the frequent thought of Mary.—*St. Teresa.*

EXAMPLE

Devotion of St. Francis de Sales to the Blessed Virgin Mary

Of all the festivals of the most holy Virgin there was none more dear to the tender piety of St. Francis de Sales than the Immaculate Conception. When but a subdeacon he instituted a confraternity of penitents, under the title of the Immaculate Conception. Every year he prepared for this feast by fasting and prayer, and his zeal induced him to proclaim this day a festival of obligation throughout his diocese. In order to place his episcopate under the protection of the Immaculate Virgin, he chose this solemnity for the day of his consecration, and during the ceremony he was rapt in ecstasy, and saw the most Holy Trinity working in his heart all that the Bishops were doing exteriorly, and moreover, he saw the most holy Virgin take him under her protection.

Once, as he was making the visitation of his diocese, he arrived at the foot of a steep and rugged hill, upon the summit of which was the church of the most Blessed Virgin of Nancy-sur-Cluses. He climbed it with great difficulty, whilst blood streamed from his feet; but in reply to those who would dissuade him from the attempt, he said: 'It is true that I am almost sinking from fatigue, but whilst I am ashamed to be so unaccustomed to labour for the service of God, I feel the greatest joy to shed my blood in honour of the Mother of God.'

Continuing his visitation he found three parish churches in succession which were dedicated to Mary. 'What a consolation I feel,' said he, 'to see so many churches in my diocese dedicated to the Mother of God! Whenever I enter a place consecrated to this august Queen, well do the beatings of my heart tell me that I am in the house of my Mother; for I am the son of her who is the refuge of sinners.'

Prayer.—O Mary! Immaculate Lily of Purity, I rejoice with you that you have been filled with grace, endowed with the use of reason, and have loved God more than the Seraphim from the first instant of your Immaculate Conception. May the most Holy Trinity be eternally thanked and adored for so many and such rare privileges bestowed upon you. I humble myself profoundly before you, seeing that I am so devoid of graces and poor in merits. O my most loving Mother, make me a partaker of the graces which you have received so abundantly, that I also may be able to love God ardently during life, and not be separated from Him in death. Amen.

Practice.—Recite three *Paters*, three *Aves*, and three *Glorias*, to thank the most Holy Trinity for the grace of the Immaculate Conception conferred upon Mary.

Aspiration.—O Mary, conceived without sin, pray for us who have recourse to you.

First Day

Mary, a Model of Perfect Self-Denial from Her Birth

LET all who are devout to the most holy Virgin approach the cradle in which lies the royal infant, Mary. Consider attentively this sacred child, and you will see how perfectly she practises every virtue. Ask the Angels, the Cherubim and Seraphim, who surround her, if they equal this little creature in perfection, and they will all reply that they are immensely inferior to her in graces, in merits, and in virtue. Contemplate, Children of Mary, those heavenly spirits around her cradle, and you will hear them repeat in ecstasies of admiration of her beauty the words of the Canticle of Canticles: *Who is she that goeth up by the desert as a pillar of smoke of aromatical spices of myrrh, and frankincense . . . Who is she that cometh forth as the morning rising, fair as the moon, bright as the sun, terrible as an army set in battle array?*

This virgin child is not yet glorified, but glory is already promised her; she expects it, not like others, in hope, but with certainty. On this account the celestial spirits, enraptured by such incomparable perfection, cease not to celebrate her praises.

Meanwhile, this most perfect Virgin lies in her poor crib, and there practises, in a most special manner, the virtue of self-abnegation. Consider, I beseech you, how, amidst angelic praises, she wishes to appear like all other children of Adam. Who will not be filled with admiration and love, to behold Mary in her cradle, full of grace, endowed with the perfect use of reason from the first instant of her Immaculate Conception, able to meditate upon the perfections of God, filled with His love, and entirely resigned to His holy will; and yet, notwithstanding such privileges, wishing to be considered and treated as a poor little infant, without in any way manifesting the precious gifts she possessed? O my God! how attractive is such a spectacle; and not only attractive, but wonderful; and how clearly does it convince us of her perfect renunciation of all that savours of worldly pomp and glory and ambition!

The second kind of abnegation which this august Virgin teaches us to practise, is the renunciation of the flesh, of which in her nativity and infancy she offers us most moving examples. Children are obliged to make many sacrifices, and the more they are attended to, the more are their affections and inclinations opposed.

These mortifications, nevertheless, are not occasions of merit to them, for they have not yet acquired the use of reason. But the most holy Virgin, being endowed from her infancy with the perfect use of reason, exercised the virtue of self-abnegation in a wonderful degree, enduring voluntarily all these contradictions and mortifications.

The third kind of renunciation is that of our own judgment and will, even in things which seem to us better than those that are commanded us. This includes what is most difficult and meritorious in the way of Christian perfection. How excellently did the most holy Virgin practise this abnegation in her nativity! Although possessed of the use of reason, she never made use of her liberty to manifest it. We always see in her a constant state of dependence. When she goes to the Temple she is led by her parents; through obedience to them she gives her hand to a humble carpenter, although she had consecrated her virginity to God. She leaves Nazareth for Bethlehem, flees into Egypt, and returns to Nazareth; and in all these journeys, as well as in all the other vicissitudes of her life, she maintains perfect subjection and docility. She even assists at the death of her Son and her God, through submission to the decrees of Heaven, her will being perfectly united to that of the Eternal Father. It was not by constraint, but with the full concurrence of her will, that she assented to the death of this Divine Son, and with humble resignation embraced and adored a hundred times that Cross upon which she saw, without shedding a tear, her only Son expire. What abnegation do we not find in the most holy Virgin! The tender loving soul of this most sorrowful Mother was pierced by unheard-of dolours; indeed, who can ever describe the pains and anguish of her most sacred heart, as she stood immovable at the foot of the Cross? She knew that the Eternal Father willed that Jesus Christ should thus die, and that she should be present at His death, and this knowledge gave her strength to stand there and endure it all.

In imitation of Mary, let us resolve to die to everything and to our own will, that we may live for God alone. Jesus Christ tells us to deny ourselves, to take up our cross and to follow Him. The way of perfection is a Calvary, where it is necessary to crucify ourselves continually, in company with our Saviour; thus forcing nature to die, that grace may live and reign within us. In a word, it is necessary to strip ourselves of the old Adam, and clothe ourselves with the new Adam, and this cannot be done without suffering. I will not deceive you; Christian perfection is difficult, and very great courage is required for so high an undertaking. This perfection consists in an entire self-abnegation, and in a total renunciation of all earthly things.[1]

O my God! when will Our Lady be, as it were, born in our hearts? As for myself I see clearly that I am quite unworthy of such a favour; and as for you, what are your sentiments? Her Divine Son was born in a stable. Let us take courage and prepare Him a place in our hearts; a place made deep by humility, low by simplicity, and wide by charity. It is such a heart as this that Our Lady loves to visit, She dwells willingly near the manger and at the foot of the Cross. Little matters it to her that she lives unknown in Egypt, provided her Divine Child lives with her.

Whether our Lord sends us to the right or to the left, or howsoever He treats us, or makes us as a sign against which all the evils of the world are turned, we will never abandon Him until He has blessed us with eternal blessing. Let us be assured that He is never so

---

1 In the way of prayer, at first everything seems painful, and with good reason; because it is a continual war against ourselves. But when we set to work, our Lord on His side assists us so powerfully, and loads us with so many favours, that all the pains and labours of this life become as nothing.—*St. Teresa*.

near to us as when He appears to be furthest from us; never does He guard us with more jealousy than when He seems to abandon us, and never does He engage in combat with us, but to take more intimate possession of our heart, and load us with His blessings. Meanwhile, let us go on; let us walk through the valley of humble virtues, and how many roses shall we not find amongst the thorns! Charity, which shines in the midst of the most trying afflictions, as well interior as exterior, the lily of purity, the violet of mortification, and how many more! But the lowly virtues that are dearest to me are these three: meekness of heart, poverty of spirit, simplicity of life, together with the practices of visiting the sick, serving the poor, consoling the afflicted, and such like. However, all must be done without solicitude, and in true liberty of spirit. Our arms are not long enough to reach to the cedars of Lebanon—let us then be content with the hyssop that grows in the valleys.

SPIRITUAL FLOWERS

There shall come forth a rod from the root of Jesse, says Isaias, and a flower shall rise up from its root. This root, writes St. Jerome, is the Mother of the Saviour; a plain and simple root, but fruitful in its unity, like the Eternal Father. The flower of this root is Jesus Christ, *like to a flower of the field and to a lily of the valley.* This flower is possessed of as many leaves as there are functions and examples. If you wish to have the flower you must first bend the stem by your prayers. If this flower rises high through the excellence of its Divinity be not afraid; because through excess of love its stem may be bowed.—*St. Bonaventure.*

I am firmly resolved to desire no other heart than that which shall be given me by this Mother of hearts, this Mother of holy love. O my God! how much do I desire not to lose sight, not even for an instant, of this gracious Star, during the whole course of my journey!—*St. Francis de Sales.*

As the lily has no fixed season for its growth, but flowers sooner or later, according to its depth in the earth, in like manner the heart which aspires to Divine Love will blossom very late, and with much difficulty, if it be absorbed in earthly cares. However, if it be attached to the world only so far as is necessary for its engagements in life, it will flourish in charity and spread around it gracious fragrance.—*The same.*

EXAMPLE

The Miraculous Medal of the Immaculate Conception

Perhaps I can relate nothing more suitable in regard to the origin of this celebrated medal, so justly styled *'miraculous,'* than by transcribing the letter addressed to the author of the book, 'Mary Conceived without Sin,' by the spiritual Director of the Sister of Charity to whom the medal was revealed:

> 'Paris, 17th March, 1834.
>
> 'Towards the close of the year 1830, Sister M., a novice of one of the communities in Paris, dedicated to the service of the Poor, saw, whilst in prayer, a picture representing the Blessed Virgin, standing with her arms extended. She wore a white garment, a blue and silver cloak, and a veil coloured like the aurora, whilst rays of dazzling splendour issued from her hands. At the same time the Sister heard these words: "These rays are the symbol of the graces which Mary obtains in favour of mankind; and that part of the globe upon which they fall with

greater abundance is France." Around the picture was written the invocation, *"O Mary, conceived without sin, pray for us who have recourse to you."* The Sister having considered it for a moment, cast her eyes upon the other side of the picture, and saw the letter *"M"* surmounted by a Cross, and below it, the Sacred Hearts of Jesus and Mary. Then the voice said again: *"A medal must be struck according to this model; and whoever shall wear it, properly blessed and indulgenced, shall be protected by the Mother of God in a most special manner,"*

'The novice came quickly to narrate the vision to me; and I, supposing it to be a mere pious illusion, simply addressed a few words to her upon true devotion to Mary, pointing out to her that the imitation of her virtues ever was, and will be, the true means of honouring her.

'After about six months, she had the same vision, and I made her the same reply. Finally, after another interval of six months, she saw the picture again, and heard the same words, except that the voice expressed how much it displeased the Blessed Virgin that there was so much delay in having the medal struck.

'"This time, however, I attached greater importance to the revelation, without allowing the novice to perceive it; and I began to reflect and fear lest I was not seconding the designs of her who is so justly invoked by the Church under the sweet name of "Refuge of Sinners."

'A short time afterwards I had the opportunity of seeing the Archbishop, and gave him an accurate account of these visions. He answered me that "he saw nothing whatever objectionable in this medal being struck, as it was conformable to the faith of the Church and to the piety of the faithful towards the Mother of God; and that it might certainly contribute to the promotion of her honour."

The medal was finally struck in the month of June, 1832.

'In one of the three visions, the novice asked if it were not necessary to insert some words on that part of the medal where the letter *"M"* and the Cross, with the two Hearts, are represented; but she was answered that these objects spoke with sufficient eloquence to the faithful soul.

'When the medal was struck, it was quickly circulated amongst the Sisters of Charity, who, when they learnt its origin, wore it with much devotion, and began to hang it on the necks of the sick under their charge, and these shortly experienced happy results. Three cures and three conversions were wrought in a miraculous manner in Paris, and in the diocese of Meaux. Then the desire to possess the *miraculous medal*, or the medal *that cures*, became universal. Mothers of families gave it as a New Year's gift to their children, and as a preservative to their innocence. As soon as it became known in a place, pious persons hastened to become possessed of it. But what greatly surprised and edified me, from the beginning of its propagation, was that all the children of two of our provinces agreed together to take this medal as the protection of their youth. In many places

> entire populations addressed themselves to their Pastor to procure it; and, at Paris, an officer purchased sixty for as many private soldiers who had asked him for it.
>
> 'Whilst the medal was miraculously propagated in all classes and provinces, the most consoling accounts were sent me by the Parish Priests, Vicar-Generals, and even by Bishops. They say that *"it reanimates fervour in populous towns as well as in the country; it gains our entire confidence; we look upon it as a means sent by Providence to enkindle faith, which in our days has so visibly decreased; and in reality it daily awakens this faith in many hearts, in which it seemed to be extinguished; it re-establishes peace and concord in many families; and there is no one who wears this medal who does not experience its salutary effects."'*

Not only in France which is specially under the protection of Mary Most Holy did the faithful of every age, sex, and condition, rival one another in zeal and solicitude to possess the *miraculous* medal; it spread also like lightning throughout Switzerland, Piedmont, Spain,

Italy, Belgium, England, America, in the Levant, and even in China; and we can certify that in the present day the number of these medals exceeds thirty millions. In every place it is asked for by indifferent Christians, by obstinate sinners, by the impious, by Protestants, Jews, and Turks, and worn with veneration. Heaven grant that it may not be without fruit!—that she, to whom the Church applies those words of Holy Scripture, *'He who shall find Me shall find life, and have salvation from the Lord,'* may conduct and confirm us in the way of salvation!

Plenary Indulgences at the hour of death, and on all the principal festivals of the year, and on the feasts of the Apostles are attached to this medal when blessed by anyone who possesses the faculty.

Prayer.—O Lovely Child, who, in your happy Nativity, didst console the world, rejoice Heaven, terrify hell, and become the relief of sinners, the consolation of the afflicted, the health of the sick, and the joy of all men, I entreat you, with all the fervour of my soul, to be spiritually born in my heart through your holy love. Attach my soul once for all to your happy service, and my heart to yours, that my life may be adorned with the virtues which will render me dear to you. O Mary!

produce in me the salutary effects of your sweet name, and obtain that the invocation of this holy name may be my strength in sufferings, my hope in dangers, my shield in spiritual conflicts, and my support and comfort in the agonies of death. May it be honey to my mouth, music to my ears, and the only joy of my heart! Amen.

Aspiration.—Morning Star, pray for me.

Practice.—Visit the altar of the Blessed Virgin, after having adored the Most Holy Sacrament of the Altar.

Second Day

Mary Consecrates Herself to God in the Temple

Mary was no sooner born than she consecrated her entire being to the service of Divine Love, and as soon as she acquired the use of her tongue she employed it in chanting the praises of the Lord. He inspired her, when she had attained the age of three years, to leave the home of her parents and retire into the Temple to serve Him more perfectly. During her tender years the life of this glorious Virgin was full of wisdom and discretion, and the cause of astonishment to her parents, for her actions and words were very different from those of other children, since she had the full use of her reason. It was therefore necessary to hasten the period for taking her to the Temple and consecrating her to the Divine service, amongst the other maidens already consecrated. They, therefore, took the little Virgin and partly led and partly carried her to the Temple of Jerusalem. Mary certainly had nothing to fear from the influences of her home, but she wished to teach us by her example that we should omit nothing, as St. Paul so earnestly teaches, to make our calling and election sure.

All who repaired to the Temple to present their offerings chanted as they went the Psalm: *Beati immaculati in via qui ambulant in lege Domini—'Blessed are the undefiled in the way, who walk in the law of the Lord'*. With what grace and melody must not our glorious Queen and Mistress have intoned this canticle when she walked towards the sanctuary where her God wished to prepare her to become, not only His Spouse, but His Mother, the blessed among all women! The very Angels were so pleased at the sight of such love, fervour, and humility, that they descended in choirs to listen to the harmony. With what joy was she not filled when she arrived at the threshhold of the Temple, and when she mounted the fifteen steps of the sanctuary! She came to dedicate herself unreservedly to God. If her youth had not forbidden it, she might thus have addressed the holy matrons who had charge of the consecrated children in the Temple: Here am I; consider me in your hands as a piece of soft wax; dispose of me as you will, I shall never make any resistance. She was so docile that she allowed herself to be guided by others in such a manner as never to show the slightest inclination to one thing more than another. She abandoned herself totally and perfectly to the Divine Will, so that she was a marvel to all who knew her.

In order to profit in a Christian manner by the example that Mary gives us in this mystery, three points can be considered: firstly, that Mary was presented to God in His Temple from her tenderest infancy, and thus separated from her parents; secondly, that she makes a great part of the journey on foot, and the rest of the journey she is carried in the arms of her parents; thirdly, that she dedicates and offers herself entirely to God, without any reserve.

As to the first point, which is to dedicate one's self to God from one's infancy, how, you will ask, can we imitate Mary in this, for we have already passed the age of childhood, and it is impossible to recover lost time? You are deceived. If virginity can be repaired by means of humility, cannot lost time be repaired by making a fervent and good use of the present? I acknowledge that the happiness of those who have dedicated themselves entirely to God from their infancy is, indeed, enviable, and He seems to receive such an offering with special complacency. He complains, through one of His prophets, that '*men had so perverted their way, that even from their youth they had abandoned the path of salvation for that of perdition.*' Children are neither good nor bad so long as they are incapable of distinguishing good from evil. But when they have attained the use of reason, too often they turn to that which is evil. Hence God says by His prophet: *Dereliquerunt me fontem aquæ vivæ—'They have forsaken Me, the fountain of living water, to follow the way of iniquity.'*

Another proof of the ardent desire of the Divine Goodness for our youthful service is found in the words of the same prophet; *Bonum est viro cum portaverit jugum ab adolescentia sua—'It is good for a man to have borne the yoke from his youth.'* But it need not be supposed that the youth of which the prophet speaks is only that of years. When the Beloved in the Canticle of Canticles turns to her Spouse and says to Him: *Oleum effusum nomen tuum, ideo adolescentulæ dilexerunt te—'Thy name is as oil poured out, therefore young maidens have loved Thee,'* do you believe she speaks of maidens who are young in years? No; but of those who are young in fervour and courage, but who have consecrated to the service of Holy Love all the moments of their life and all the affections of their hearts.

It is the present time, the present moment, that we should turn to profit; because the past has escaped us, and the future is not in our power. But you ask, How can we repair lost time? You can do it by the use of fervour and diligence during the time that remains for your pilgrimage upon earth. Stags do not always run at an extraordinary speed, but yet, when pursued by the hunter, they quicken their movement and seem rather to fly than to run. This is a model for us. We must not only run, but fly in the way of perfection. Therefore let us, with holy David, beg our Lord to give us *the wings of a dove*, that we may fly without stopping, until we gain our hiding-place in the walls of the holy city of Jerusalem; that is to say, until we find ourselves united to our Lord crucified upon Calvary, through an entire and perfect mortification of all our inclinations and affections.

Oh, how happy are those souls who follow the example of this Sacred Virgin, and dedicate themselves from their tender years to the service of God! Fortunate are they to have retired from the world before they were known to it! Like delicate flowers scarcely yet open, nor touched by the heat of concupiscence, they exhale a most sweet odour in the Divine Presence by means of their virtues and innocence.

SPIRITUAL FLOWERS

Mary was like a most beautiful flower, which diffuses its perfume from its very first budding. Flowers differ in their method of diffusing fragrance, as, for instance, roses and carnations. Roses smell sweeter in the morning before mid-day; but carnations and pinks shed a more pleasing scent in the evening. The glorious Virgin was like a most beautiful rose amongst thorns, and although never for an instant did she cease to diffuse an odour of surpassing sweetness, yet the fragrance of her infancy was the most acceptable to the Divine Majesty.—*St. Francis de Sales.*

Chastity is the lily of virtues, because it renders men equal to the Angels; if virtues be separated from purity, they are no longer virtues. Purity is chastity, and it possesses a glory of its own, for it clothes both soul and body with its beauty.—*The same.*

As the busy bee flies to all the flowers, and sucks from each its purest juice with which to form honey, so should a religious soul observe the virtues of others, and learn, for instance, modesty from one, science from another, and obedience from a third; in a word, he should take from each one that which he perceives to be most perfect, and copy it in his own person.—*St. Antony.*

EXAMPLE

The Two Invocations of St. Philip Neri

Of the many prayers of aspiration of St. Philip Neri to the Most Holy Virgin, two were very familiar to him. The first was, 'Virgin Mary, Mother of God, pray to Jesus for us'; the second consisted in the two words, 'Virgin and Mother'. He used to say that they contain all the panegyrics of Mary, both because they express her admirable name, and because they declare her two miraculous privileges of *Virginity* and *Maternity*, and the incomparable title of *Mother of God.* He composed a rosary with these two invocations, which he recited frequently with his penitents, and had always in his hands.

A pious person, who was continually tormented by evil thoughts, asked him one day for a remedy. The Saint counselled her to recite this rosary of his, which consisted in repeating these two invocations alternately, sixty-three times. She followed his advice, and in a short time recovered her peace of soul.

Prayer of St. Gertrude.—O Mary, Mother of Jesus, and my own dear Mother! clothe me with the fleece of the true Lamb, your Son Jesus, that His love may receive me, nourish me, possess me, and sanctify me. Shining Lily, my only hope, after God, deign to speak to your Beloved Son in my favour; say an efficacious word to Him, and faithfully and earnestly plead my cause. I beseech you, O my Mother! by your love for Jesus, to accept me as your child; be solicitous for my welfare throughout the whole course of my life, and especially at the hour of my death take me entirely under your protection. Amen.

Aspiration.—Mary, Virgin and Mother! make me a Saint.

Practice.—Let all your actions this day be done in union with Jesus and Mary.

Third Day

Continuation of the Preceding Subject

The second point presented to our consideration in the presentation of Our Lady is that in order to consecrate herself to God in the Temple she was carried part of the way by her parents, and walked the remainder, being, however, always assisted by them. When St. Joachim and St. Anne arrived at a spot where the road was level they placed the little maiden on the ground, and allowed her to walk, but even then she lifted up her little hands to clasp theirs, that she might not stumble, and when they came to the rougher parts of the road they again took her in their arms. It should not be supposed that the intentions of her parents in allowing her to walk was to relieve themselves; they allowed it because of the satisfaction which they experienced in seeing their little daughter directing her first steps to the Temple of the Lord.

Now, it is in these two ways that our Lord leads His faithful servants in their pilgrimage through this miserable life. At times He conducts us by the hand, making us walk with Him; and very often He carries us in the arms of His Providence. He leads us by the hand when He makes us walk along the path of the exercise of virtues, because if He did not help us it would be impossible for us to take one step along this blessed road. And do we not perceive that the steps of those who have abandoned the paternal hand of Providence are almost always so many falls? The Divine Goodness wishes to lead us by the hand along our road, but He also wishes us to make use of our feet; that is to say, that we ourselves do all that is in our power, by the assistance of His grace. Therefore Holy Church, like a tender mother desirous of the good of her children, teaches us to recite daily a prayer by which we beg God to deign to accompany us during the whole course of our pilgrimage upon this earth, and to succour us by His preventing and by His accompanying grace, because without both these graces all our efforts to make one step in the way of virtue would be unavailing.

But after our Lord has led us by the hand along the road of good works which require our co-operation in order that they may become meritorious, He carries us in His arms, producing certain effects within us, in which we seem to take no part, as, for instance, in the Sacraments. Tell me candidly, what is it that we do in order to merit the reception of the Most Holy Sacrament of the Altar, which contains all the sanctity and sweetness of heaven and earth? Does not our Lord carry us in His arms in permitting us to receive Him in this Sacrament?

Oh, how happy are those souls who so pass through this mortal life as never to leave the arms of His Divine Majesty, except to do all in their power to labour in the practice of virtue, still keeping hold of the hand of their Lord! Let us never believe ourselves capable of doing the least good of ourselves. The Sacred Spouse of the Canticles teaches us this truth when she says to her Beloved: *Trahe me post Te in odorem curremus unguentorum tuorum—'Draw me, and we will run after thee to the odour of thy ointments.'* She says '*draw me*,' to teach us that our soul can do nothing of itself unless it be drawn, assisted, and anticipated by Divine Grace. But to show us that she corresponds voluntarily to this attraction, she quickly adds: '*We will run*,' as if she wished to say: If only, my Beloved, Thou stretch out Thy hand to draw me, I shall not cease to run, until Thou hast received me into Thine arms, and united me to Thy Divine Will.

Let us now pass to the third point: the consecration and dedication our glorious Lady made of her whole self unreservedly to the Divine Majesty; it is this, O faithful souls, that we should try to imitate. Our Lord does not certainly expect us to be more liberal to Him than He is to us; nevertheless, if He shows the greatness of His goodness to us by giving us His whole Self, is it not just that He should require of us the total dedication of ourselves to Him? But what means this total dedication of ourselves to God? It means that we make no reserve whatever in our consecration, not even of the least of our affections or desires; it is this that He requires of us. Listen, in fact, to this Divine Saviour of our souls: *Fili præte mihi cor tuum—'My Son,'* says He to each one of us in particular—*'My Son, give Me thy heart.'* 'Ah!' you will add, 'how shall I dare to give my heart to God when it is so full of imperfections and sins? How can He accept the offering of this heart in which He finds nothing but disobedience to His Most Holy Will?' Ah! be not troubled on this account, but offer it to Him all the same, because He does not require of you a pure and spotless heart, like that of the Angels and of Our Lady, but He says: 'Give Me thy heart,' such as it is. Ah! let us not refuse it to Him then, although it be full of miseries, weaknesses, and imperfections, for we know that all that is placed in the hand of His Divine Goodness is converted into good. Let us not fear, then, for when He holds this heart of ours in His hands He will know well how to render it perfect. To make it less unworthy of God let us resolve to imitate Mary; for amongst all the Saints who are proposed to us as a model we should in a special manner consider our most glorious and dear Patroness, the Queen of all Saints. What mirror more beautiful, more precious, or purer, can we place before our eyes? Is she not the most excellent example of evangelical teaching? Who amongst creatures is more adorned and enriched with every kind of virtue and grace? *Multæ filiæ congregaverunt divitias, tu supergressa es universus—'Many daughters have gathered riches, but thou hast surpassed them all.'* Certainly it is beyond all doubt that there is no Saint comparable to her, because this glorious Virgin surpasses in dignity and excellence not only the greatest Saints, but the very Cherubim and Seraphim. She consecrated herself perfectly to the Divine service, from the very first instant of her Immaculate Conception.

SPIRITUAL FLOWERS

When the senses are not well guarded, they are mysterious inlets by which our enemies insinuate themselves into our souls. A glance of curiosity changed holy King David into an adulterer and a murderer. How many have reason to exclaim with Jeremiah, *'My eye hath been the thief that has robbed my soul of every good'!—Riva.*

The choice of a state of life is so important that it constitutes the only foundation of a good or of a bad life.—*St. Greg. Naz.*

The Christian who abandons himself into the hand of God, lives for God alone.—*St. Francis de Sales.*

EXAMPLE

The Feasts of the Blessed Virgin

The days upon which the Blessed Virgin Mary shows herself bountiful of her favours, are the feasts celebrated in her honour; and if we desire to profit by them, we must sanctify them fervently. Let us approach the Sacraments on those days, and propose to practise some particular virtue of the Blessed Virgin, adapted to the mystery of the day. For instance, on the Feast of the Immaculate Conception, let us propose to practise purity of intention; on that of her Nativity, a renewal of fervour, banishing all tepidity from our soul; on that of the Presentation, detachment from those desires which require to be mortified; on the Feast of the Annunciation, of the Visitation, on the Feast of the Purification, obedience to Superiors; and on the Feast of the Assumption, preparation for death. Such was ever the practice of all the true servants of Mary; amongst others, of St. Bernardine of Siena, of St. Gertrude, and of St. Vincent Ferrer.

Mary herself made known to St. Gertrude, as we read in the tenth chapter of the 'Revelations' of this Saint, that she rewards this practice with every kind of favour. On the Feast of the Assumption, whilst the Divine Sacrifice of the Mass was being celebrated, the Blessed Virgin showed the Saint a great number of young girls, whom she carefully guarded under her rich mantle. 'My dear daughter,' said she to her, 'behold here those souls who do all in their power to celebrate this festival worthily.'

Brother Gerard, one of the first lay-brothers of the Congregation of St. Alfonso de Liguori, had the most tender confidence in Mary. At the approach of her feasts he took care to adorn all the altars of the monastery, and his devotion was especially great to the Immaculate Conception. He wished that the faithful would fast on all the vigils of her feasts; on which days his nourishment was but a little bread and water, and he gave himself the discipline to blood. During all her novenas, he performed some abstinence or good work in her honour. When he was allowed by his Superior, he spent the night preceding her festivals prostrate before her altar in fervent prayer. It is narrated by Fathers Petrella and Giovenale that the Blessed Virgin, touched by the love of her servant, appeared to him during one of those nights, and enriched him with favours of many kinds.

Prayer of St. Gertrude to the Sacred Heart of Mary.—O Immaculate Heart of Mary, I have nothing to offer you that is worthy of you; yet how many thanks should I not render you for all the favours that you have obtained for me from the Heart of Jesus! What reparation should I not offer you for my languor during Divine service! I would wish to render you love for love: the only good that I possess is the Sacred Heart of Jesus, which you have yourself given to me. I offer you, then, this treasure of infinite value—I can do nothing more, and nothing less do you merit from me. Accept, then, this gift, which is so dear to you; and nothing more do I desire except that you will deign to accept, also, my poor heart. Amen.

Aspiration.—Mother of Good Counsel, pray for me.

Practice.—Make a sincere act of contrition for the time that you have spent away from God.

Fourth Day

Fidelity of Mary in Following the Call of God

Let us consider in this meditation the punctual care with which Mary always followed her vocation.

God had uttered in her ears, or rather in the interior of her heart, the words of the psalm: *Audi Fili, inclina aurem tuam, et obliviscere populum tuum, et domum patris tui et concupiscet rex decorem tuum*—'*Hearken, my child, incline thine ear to Me; forget thy people and thy father's house, and the King shall desire thy beauty.*'

Ponder attentively these words: '*Hearken, child*'—*Audi Fili*. They imply that, in order to hear well, it is necessary to listen, first, very attentively—'*inclina aurem tuam*;' it is to the humble alone that God deigns to make known His Will. '*Forget thy people and thy fathers house, and the King will greatly desire thy beauty.*' This is as if He would say, do not confine thyself to listening to the word of inspiration, and abasing thyself in order that thou mayest understand it, but further strip thy heart of all affection for thy country and thy relations, and then I shall be delighted with thy beauty. O, holy and Divine seed which our Lord sows in the hearts of so many! And yet how many there are who hear the Divine call, without making one step to leave their country and go whither God calls them! Diligence is taken to examine and consider attentively whether the inspiration comes from God, or from the enemy of all good, or if it be the deception of self-love; and meanwhile, through our own fault, the Divine vocation fails in its effect. I do not wish to condemn the considerations which ought to be made in order to discern well the nature of the inspiration. By no means; but after having made your examen with simplicity, in the presence of God, and recognised His voice, go forth quickly and enter the land which He points out to you. Listen no longer to so many discourses and reasonings suggested by the spirit of the world, because procrastination under such circumstances exposes you to very serious dangers. Do not, then, lull yourself to sleep, but follow diligently the Divine attraction.

With what assiduity and with what solicitude did not the glorious Virgin obey the sacred call of God! She had no need of protracted self-examination, because she was endowed with the grace of discernment. Therefore, although but a child, she repaired without delay whither her God led her, and the King of Heaven, won by her beauty, chose her not only for His Spouse, but also for His Mother. '*Blessed are they that hear the word of God and keep it.*'

Certainly, all are not called to follow the same path, and yet they may all follow the Divine inspirations. We will explain. The Church may be considered as the Court of a great Prince or King, in whose kingdom are many vassals or under-lords. All these vassals are invited to Court, and all share in the favours of their Sovereign, but differently. Some are favoured in a very special manner, and He treats them with greater confidence than the rest, and repeats to them His secrets. But besides the graces which He grants in general to all the members of His Church, to some amongst them He bestows more precious favours; for instance, religious persons, whom He admits into His Cabinet—that is to say, into holy religion—in order to entertain Himself with them familiarly, and disclose His secrets to them in the closest union of Heart.

Amongst those who have received this grace, the Most Holy Virgin has been singularly privileged, Our Lord having made known to her secrets and mysteries which have been revealed to no other creature. Happy was she to have heard the word of God and kept it, and how happy also will you be, pious souls, if you endeavour, in imitation of her, to follow promptly the inspirations by which God manifests to you His Most Holy Will!

I am well aware that for many it is necessary that they should live in the world. These persons should use, but not abuse the riches, honours and dignities which they are allowed by the law of God to possess; and if they endeavour, in the use of these possessions, to conform their affections to the commandments of God, without following the counsels, they will be as truly blessed, and will attain to the joys of eternal life.

There are many persons who wish to consecrate themselves to God, but at the same time wish to reserve always something for themselves. They will say, for instance, I will give to God what belongs to God, and reserve for the world what is due to the world, without however doing what would be an offence to His Divine Majesty, or contrary to His most holy law. Such as these listen, it is true, to the inspirations of God, but do not correspond to them with their whole heart, and although they may be saved, yet they never will reach a high degree of perfection and glory.

There are others who are quite resolved to follow steadily the inspirations and Will of God, and also desire to live united to Him, but not in a *perfect manner*.

Observe well that there is a great difference between being *all* given to God and *wholly* given to God. These persons of whom we speak wish to reserve to themselves the choice at least of their spiritual exercises, in order, as they say, that they may the better serve God. But to how much danger of being deceived do not they expose themselves! Regulating themselves according to their own notions, they refuse to submit to others, and they mark out for themselves a mode of life according to their own caprices. I would say to such souls: Do you not perceive that with these ideas you do not belong *wholly* to God? Their answer would be: But I act so in order to serve God. But this is not the example that our most Blessed Lady, the glorious Virgin, gives us. On the day of her presentation she consecrated herself to God entirely, without any reserve, and never again made use of her own will or choice. O faithful souls, you ought continually to keep before your eyes the life of our dear Lady, and meditate upon it, so as to be able to conform all your actions and affections to this perfect model. You are her children, and therefore you ought to follow her, to imitate her, and make use of her as a mirror in which you should always view and study yourselves well. The sweetness which will flow from the consideration of her virtues will be received in earthen vessels; nevertheless, its fragrance will be none the less sweet. The balsam that is contained in an earthen vase is as sweet as that in a vase of crystal.

SPIRITUAL FLOWERS

Most yellow flowers keep turned continually to the sun, but the sunflower turns not only its flowers but also its leaves towards the great luminary. In like manner the elect turn the flower of their hearts—that is, their obedience—to the commands of God's will.—*St. Francis de Sales.*

The virtues of the friends of God are ennobled and raised to the dignity of holy works by the excellence of the heart which produces them. All their virtuous actions are dedicated to God, for how can a heart that has given Him itself not give to Him all that belongs to it? Does not he who gives a whole tree give also the leaves, and flowers, and fruit?—*The same.*

The rose possesses the property of killing by its odour all the snails that come around it. Similarly, the devout soul, who is as a rose before God, should chase away and destroy all the creeping things that gather around her heart—that is to say, the coldness and tepidity which are an obstacle to her advancement in the way of God.—*The same.*

EXAMPLE

Lamps and Candles Burnt in Honour of Mary

It is a custom amongst Catholics to have lamps or candles burning upon altars, or before pictures of the august Mother of God for one, or three, or nine consecutive days, so as to obtain spiritual or temporal favours. This touching practice, springing from the love of Mary, comes down from the remotest antiquity. Oil and wax, as all know, have a deep signification. The flame is a symbol of the vivacity of our faith and of the firmness of our confidence; fire symbolizes the ardour of charity, and the ascent of the flame is a type of our hope. These flames intimate that we must keep the fire of charity ever burning in our hearts, so as to be always ready to receive our Divine Master whensoever He shall call us to the nuptials of the Lamb. Lamps lighted before the statues or pictures of Mary represent to us more specially the prayer of intercession, which goes direct to the Heart of God. They awaken a singular emotion in the heart of him who has faith. The oil that feeds the flame has often cost the poor man the sweat of hard labour, but he thinks little of this voluntary sacrifice, because it was the fruit of love. No one who has not visited Italy, and in particular Rome and Naples, can form an idea of the honour that is paid to the Blessed Virgin. You will find her image on all the roadsides, in the public squares, houses and shops, with lamps, often many at a time, burning before them, and the amount of oil that is consumed in this manner is considerable. This is a voluntary contribution of the poor as well as of the rich, and it is an expense that every pious family considers as necessary as their daily bread. At Rome there exists a sweet custom of writing a short prayer, often with the indulgence attached to its repetition, under each image or picture, and it is repeated by the passers-by. Who can say how many passions are repressed, how many unhappy creatures consoled, and how many hopes aroused by this short invocation?

Prayer of St. Germanus.—O you, who are, after God, my powerful protectress and my true consolation in this world, you who are the celestial dew that sweetens my pains; the light of my soul when plunged in darkness, my guide in my journeys, my strength in my weaknesses, my treasure in poverty, the remedy of my wounds, my joy in all my sorrows, my refuge in all dangers, the hope of my life and of my salvation, deign to hear my prayers, to take an interest in my woes, and to show me that compassion which peculiarly belongs to the Mother of a God Who entertains such love and goodness towards men. He is their Father, and He has constituted you their Mother. Ah! place me then amongst the number of your dearest children, and obtain for me from God all the graces which you know to be necessary for the salvation of my soul. Amen.

Aspiration.—O Mary! be my guiding star.

Practice.—Examine what has been your fidelity in following your vocation, and how its obligations have been fulfilled.

Fifth Day

Mary Is a Model to Religious Persons in Her Presentation in the Temple

God had commanded all the Hebrews to visit the Temple, but all, rich and poor, were forbidden to enter it empty-handed: *Non apparetis in conspectu meo vacuus*. The offering, however, was not the same for all. The rich were to give according to their riches, the poor according to their poverty, and thus all were able to observe the precept. From this we may understand that when seculars come to God and offer Him the desire and will, they entertain to follow and observe His Divine commandments. He will be satisfied with this offering, and if they put it in practice faithfully, they will obtain eternal life. But let those souls who are rich in means for doing great things for the glory of God, such as religious persons, beware lest they present themselves with the offering of the poor—that is, of seculars; for God will not be satisfied with such an offering. Our Lord, in calling you, my dear sisters, into Holy Religion, enriched you with His graces, and on this account He requires much from you; that is, He will have your offering to be of all that you are, and of all that you possess, without any reserve.

The Blessed Virgin, in her Presentation, made an offering pleasing to God; offered not only the dignity of her person (the most excellent amongst pure creatures), but all that she possessed. How happy are the Religious who, by means of their vows, have consecrated all to God, dedicating to Him their bodies, their hearts, and all that they possess; renouncing riches by the vow of poverty, pleasures by the vow of chastity, and their whole will by the vow of obedience! Worldlings, you may enjoy your riches if you will, but do not abuse them, nor wrong anyone. The pleasures that Holy Church permits are lawful; you are not prohibited in a thousand circumstances from following your own will, provided it be not contrary to that of God. But you, Religious, should offer all to God, without any reserve. He wishes your offering to be entire, such as is the gift He makes to you of Himself in the Divine Sacrament of the Altar. Forget not that you cannot deceive Him, and if you say that you wish to consecrate yourselves perfectly to His Divine Majesty, and do not really do so, you are in danger of being punished like Ananias and Sapphira, who lied to the Holy Ghost.

Now, the Blessed Virgin was always perfectly obedient to the Will of God, from the first instant of her conception, without ever changing or suspending for a moment the resolution she had formed to serve Him.

Do we not daily experience how changeable is man in his good resolutions? How often, even in one hour, do we not like and dislike the same thing, and allow ourselves to be moved by excessive joy or excessive sadness! This was not the case with Our Lady; she hourly became more perfectly united to God, and merited fresh graces, and the more she received, the more did she render her soul worthy to receive them. By these means she was always strengthening her first resolution, so that the only change that could have been perceptible in her was the progress she made from one degree of perfection to another, through the practice of every virtue. It was for this purpose that she wished to retire into the Temple, not through any need she had of this retreat, for her perseverance was assured by her consecration at the first moment of her existence, but in order to instruct us, who are so changeable and inconstant, that it is our duty to make use of every means in our power to strengthen and preserve our good resolutions.

Imitate the Most Holy Virgin also in this. Dedicate, therefore, yourselves entirely to God; and whenever you renew your consecration, you will acquire new strength and vigour in the service of His Divine Majesty. Renew your resolutions, renew them frequently and with fidelity, to the end of your life. This was the careful practice of all the Saints of both the Old and of the New Testament. Our nature is of itself weak and easily depressed when there is a question of virtuous resolutions. The earth itself has its periods of weakness, and refuses to be always yielding its produce; so it lies barren in winter. But when the spring arrives it renews itself, and having recovered fresh vigour, it gives us the benefit of its fruits.

For this reason Holy Church, like a wise Mother, puts before us from time to time, during the course of the year, special festivals, to animate us to renew our good resolutions. Who will not renew his soul on the solemn festivals of Easter, Pentecost, and Christmas, by holy affections and firm resolutions to live more virtuously? But besides the observance of all these festivals, it has ever been a laudable custom for persons more especially consecrated to God, such as Religious, to choose one day in particular during the course of the year upon which to renew their vows, and by so doing to obey the great Apostle, who counsels us to confirm our vocation.

Divine Providence has permitted for our instruction, that Our Lady should renew in her Presentation the sacrifice which she had made of her whole self at the moment of her Immaculate Conception. Do you, then, religious souls, make this renewal in imitation of her, and do it with great fervour of spirit, with profound humility, and ardent charity. Place your hearts, your souls, and your entire being in the hands of this Holy Virgin; she will present you to the Most Holy Trinity, and you will obtain a thousand blessings in this life, and will be enabled to arrive at eternal glory in the next.

NOTE: It is an ancient and well-grounded tradition that Mary was led to the Temple to be presented to the Lord at three years of age, and that she dwelt in that sacred abode until the age of fourteen that is to say, as long as was permitted by the laws of the Sanhedrim. St. Bonaventure relates to us the life led by the Most Holy Virgin in that voluntary retirement. 'We may learn,' says this Father, 'what Mary did in the Temple from her own revelations to one of her faithful servants, supposed to be St. Elizabeth.' Amongst other things we read as follows: 'As soon as I was left in the Temple by my parents, I determined in my heart to look upon God as my Father. I often considered what I could do to merit His grace, and I began to instruct myself in His holy law. But of all the Divine precepts, these three principally occupied my attention: (1) Thou shalt love the Lord thy God with thy whole heart, with all thy soul, and with all thy strength; (2) thou shalt love thy neighbour as thyself; (3) thou shalt hate thy enemy.

'I kept the commandments in my heart, and I quietly embraced all the virtues that they contain. It is thus that I wish you to conduct yourself. In fact, the soul can possess no virtue whatever if it do not love God with all its powers, because it is from this love alone that the fulness of grace (without which virtue will never be preserved in the soul) descends to us; but it will pass like running water and vanish if the *soul hates not its enemies*, which are *sin and vice*. He who desires to acquire and preserve grace must accustom his heart, then, to the exercise of this love and of this hatred, and it is in this that I wish to be imitated by you.'

The faithful servant of Mary, having heard these words, replied: 'My sweetest Lady, wast thou not already full of grace and virtue?' The Blessed Virgin replied: 'Be certain that I believed myself to be the vilest sinner, and, like you, unworthy of grace. You perhaps believe, my daughter, that all the grace which I possessed was acquired without difficulty. But it was not so. On the contrary, I received no grace or favour without constant prayer, ardent desire, deep devotion, and many tears, with long afflictions, excepting, however, the grace of sanctification, which was given to me from my conception in my mother's womb, and, as far as I knew, I never said or thought of anything but what was pleasing to my God.' She added: 'Be assured also that no grace descends into the soul, except through the channel of prayer and corporal mortification. But as soon as we have given to God all that we possess, He Himself comes quickly to dwell within us, bringing with Him such inestimable gifts that the soul feels her heart to fail; she loses the remembrance of having ever done or said anything acceptable to God, and she becomes more and more vile and contemptible in her own eyes.'—*Maria Regina e Madre Dei Santi*, by l'Abate Guyard, Vic. Gen. of Montalbano.

SPIRITUAL FLOWERS

Flowers fade quickly if they are much handled, but if they are not touched they may be preserved a long time.—*À Kempis.*

The root of the plant is hidden under ground and trodden under foot; it has neither odour nor beauty, and yet it gives life to the flower. Thus a humble soul may, like Mary, be despised, it may be trodden upon, forgotten; but this is the way for it to produce flowers and fruits for eternal life.—*Nouet.*

The lily is the symbol of chastity; it preserves its whiteness and sweetness in the midst of thorns, so long as it is left untouched, but as soon as ever it is plucked it emits so overpowering an odour that it causes headache.—*St. Francis de Sales.*

Whiteness is not an essential property of the rose—indeed, red roses are more beautiful and of sweeter odour; but it is the property of the lily. Let us endeavour to be what we are, and as justly and perfectly as possible, that we may do honour to our Maker.—*The same.*

EXAMPLE

The Edifying Death of St. Jane Frances de Chantal

It was on the Feast of the Immaculate Conception of Mary that this Saint was attacked by the first serious symptoms of her fatal illness. On the eve of the feast she was in the refectory, and after the blessing of the table she knelt down, and with her arms in the form of a cross repeated twice these words: *O Mater Dei, memento mei*. She then commented upon these words thus: 'Holy Mother of God, by your Immaculate Conception, remember me and assist me always, especially at the hour of my death.' She remained for a long time afterwards in the same posture, absorbed in profound recollection.

The following day she was confined to her bed to rise no more. Her illness increasing every hour, she knew that her end approached, and thought only of preparing herself to appear before God. She received the last Sacraments with striking fervour, and preserved her calmness and serenity amidst the tears and sobs of all the community. During her intense sufferings she was heard to address the following prayer to the Most Holy Virgin: 'O Mary, Mother of Grace, Mother of Mercy, defend me from the snares of the infernal enemy, and receive my soul into your hands at the moment of my death.' She kept a picture of her Protectress always near her bed; and when her speech failed she made great efforts to turn her eyes frequently towards this dear picture, and before she breathed her last asked to kiss it once more, and to have it buried with her in the tomb.

Prayer.—O Mary, the purest of Virgins! terrified at my weakness and at the dangers that surround me, I recommend to thy loving care with all confidence the chastity of my soul and body. Permit me not, O Queen of the Angels, to be defiled by the least stain after having been adorned with purity and innocence, like a vessel of honour and glory. Banish from my heart all sensual desires, evil thoughts, and irregular affections. To thy love, O my good Mother, do I confide my heart; purify it, render it worthy to be offered to thy Beloved Son, that, having here on earth imitated thee in the most beautiful of thy virtues, I may enjoy with thee for ever in heaven the happiness promised to the clean of heart. Amen.

Aspiration.—Grant, O my God, that through Mary I may belong entirely to Jesus!

Practice.—If you should meet with any contradiction today, preserve your peace of soul.

Sixth Day

The Annunciation of the Most Holy Virgin

We read in the Gospel that the Angel Gabriel visited Our Lady in the town of Nazareth; and, as the word 'Nazareth' signifies 'flowers,' well is the Church represented in this town! What, in fact, is the Church but a house or a town adorned with flowers? All actions performed according to her laws are as so many flowers. Mortifications, humiliations, prayers—in short, all pious exercises are acts of virtue, which, like most beautiful flowers, diffuse a pleasing fragrance before God. Most justly, then, may we call the Christian religion a garden of flowers, that are delightful to the sight and most salutary to those who breathe the air impregnated by their fragrance. Our Lady herself was a flower distinguished for beauty and excellence above all other flowers—a flower of incomparable fragrance, possessed of the power of producing many other flowers: *Hortus conclusus, soror mea, sponsa—'Thou,'* says the sacred Spouse in the Canticles, *'art a garden enclosed:'* a garden all studded with the most magnificent flowers that can be produced. Now, tell me to whom belong so many charming and sweet-scented flowers, with which the Church is so gloriously adorned, but to the Most Holy Virgin, since they were produced by her example? It is through her that Holy Church is so well furnished with roses in the martyrs who were invincible in their constancy; with every kind of flower, in the confessors who were nursed in her bosom; and with sweet violets, in so many holy widows, who lowly, humble, and hidden, diffuse the most odoriferous sweetness. In fine, is it indeed not to her that belong, in a special manner, so many lilies of purity and spotless virginity, innocent souls, bright and clear as a resplendent mirror? There can be no doubt, that if so many virgins have consecrated their hearts and bodies to His Divine Majesty, by indissoluble vows, it was that they might imitate the example of the Most Holy Virgin.

She was the first to consecrate her body, her heart, and her whole self to God, by the vow of virginity. Hardly had she been *drawn* by God than she quickly drew after her a large number of souls who consecrated themselves to God in like manner, under her sacred auspices, in order that they might run in the way of inviolable chastity and virginity: *Adducentur regi virgines post eam*. You, beloved souls, were seen by the glorious Virgin, when she exclaimed: *Curremus*—'*We shall run,* thus assuring her Beloved that many would follow her standard, and that under her protection they might combat and vanquish every kind of enemy.

What an honour for us to be able to walk under the standard of the Queen of Virgins! Our Lady is undoubtedly the honour, the Protectress, and model of all Christians, of men and women of all classes who live virtuously; yet, undoubtedly, young virgins contract by their virginity a closer alliance with her than other Christians, for their resemblance to her in purity enables them more easily and more closely to approach her.[2]

It is said that when the Angel came down from heaven to venerate the spotless Virgin, and announce to her the Incarnation of the Son of God in her most chaste womb, she was alone in her room. Faithful souls are here instructed to have a love of retirement from the world, but this is not enough; they ought also to retire

2 *It is the opinion of a Doctor of the Church that the Holy Virgin Mary instituted some congregations of young girls, and that when she lived at Ephesus with the Apostle St. John she gave rules and constitutions to one of them. How happy were those Religious to have been instituted by the Queen of Doctors, who gathered her wisdom from her Son, who is the Wisdom of the Eternal Father!*—'Month of Mary.' *St. Francis de Sales.*

within themselves that they may lead a solitary life, and thus render themselves better prepared to enjoy the conversation of their Beloved. Each should look upon his heart as a celestial cabinet where he lives alone with Him. O faithful souls, if you conceal yourselves thus, the Angels will know how to find you, as the Archangel Gabriel found Mary because she was alone.

Nothing should be so pleasing to holy virgins and to true Religious as this state of withdrawal, because they then contemplate better the beauty of their Divine Spouse dwelling in the depths of their hearts. On this account the Psalmist said that 'All the beauty of the King's Daughter is within'—*Omnis gloria filiæ regis ab intus*. The greatest diligence is necessary to preserve and increase this interior beauty, and at the same time to guard it continually from everything that could tarnish it, remembering that although men see only the exterior, the Divine Spouse penetrates into the inmost recesses of the heart. This is the motive which induces the loving spouse (I speak of a soul consecrated to the Divine service, in order to please God alone), to live retired within her own heart, and thus prepare an acceptable abode for His Divine Majesty. It is on this account that solitude is so much recommended to religious persons; its utility is seen by the diligence with which Our Lady practised it, and which merited for her the sublime privilege of being chosen to be the Mother of God!

Our Lord being the only rest of those who have abandoned all worldly cares in order to listen to Him speaking to their hearts in solitude, it follows that if they do not attend to the interior word of Jesus Christ that solitude becomes a long martyrdom to them. Instead of being the habitation of peace and tranquillity their solitude is a cause of sadness and disquiet.

Those who lead like Martha a life of great activity may still enjoy the tranquillity of Mary, if they are careful to refer all their works to God: this *one aim* being *the eye which touches the heart of the Divine Spouse*. In order not to lose the security of our habitation, we must seek it, not so much in a *cell*, as in *God Himself*. Thrice happy are they who dwell in this House, which not only belongs to God, but is God Himself, for He will be their abiding rest throughout ages of ages.

SPIRITUAL FLOWERS

Whatever flower the bee rests upon, it always extracts honey from it. So will it be with an interior soul: if she never leave her home but when it is necessary for the glory of God, she will always return to it laden with the honey of good works.—*A Father of the Desert.*

When grace speaks it is time to act, not to hold discourse. Long prayers unaccompanied by mortification are nothing in the sight of God, but time spent uselessly.—*St. Teresa.*

Whoever abandons prayer casts himself into hell.—*The same.*

Holy prayer is a water of benediction, which refreshes the plants of our good desires and makes them flourish. It washes our souls from their imperfections, and extinguishes the fire of passion in our hearts.—*St. Francis de Sales.*

EXAMPLE

St. Bernard's Love for Mary

The luminous star of the Middle Ages, St. Bernard, who was the soul of the Crusades instituted for the defence of religion and of civilized Europe, the counsellor of Bishops, Popes, and Kings, may be said to have had infused into him at his baptism a special devotion to the Most Holy Virgin. In his tenderest infancy he leaped for joy when he saw by chance a picture of Mary, or when he heard her name pronounced. He was ever thinking of her, and wished everyone to be speaking to him always of her. To correct in him those defects which are common to childhood, it sufficed to tell him that such and such a thing was displeasing to Mary, and he immediately took care not to repeat the fault, and he eagerly embraced those practices of piety which he was told were dear to her. She, on her side, did not delay to manifest the care she took of him, and undoubtedly the great love he had for holy purity was a special gift from the Queen of Virgins. Other favours, however, were in store for him in the hands of his powerful benefactress.

On Christmas Eve the young Bernard was waiting in the church with his relations for the commencement of the midnight service, when, having inclined his head, he fell into a kind of ecstasy, and saw in spirit, by means of supernatural light, the mystery of Bethlehem, and he quietly contemplated the Divine Infant miraculously born from the virginal womb of His Mother. This vision penetrated him with so warm a feeling of gratitude towards Jesus and Mary, that he immediately promised to consecrate himself entirely to their love and service henceforth. The writings of St. Bernard breathe a tender piety towards Mary, and unite all the most beautiful and moving expressions of love and veneration for her, which were written in former ages, and he united in his heart all the affections of the most zealous of her servants. With what respect, confidence, and love towards this good Mother are we penetrated when we read the pious works that he has written for her glory! His emotion, when under the influence of these sentiments, frequently rapt him in ecstasy.

Prayer of St. Andrew of Crete.—Hail, Mary, full of grace, the Lord is with you! Hail you, O source of our joy! through you the sentence of our condemnation was changed into a sentence of benediction! Hail, O Temple of the glory of God, sacred dwelling of the King of the heavenly kingdom! You are truly blessed amongst all women, because you were chosen to be the Mother of your Creator, and all nations shall call you blessed.

O Mary, I place in you a holy confidence, and from you I expect my salvation. I shall walk without fear in the midst of all my enemies, if you will deign to number me amongst those whom you protect. Sincere love of you is the safest weapon with which to fight and overcome; number me, then, amongst your children, for I have chosen you for my tender Mother. Amen.

Aspiration.—Sub tuum præsidium confugimus, sancta Dei Genitrix—We put ourselves under your powerful protection, O Holy Mother of God!

Practice.—Recite today the *Angelus* with great fervour.

Seventh Day

The Excellence of the Virginity of Mary

Let us consider attentively the virtues that were practised by the Most Holy Virgin on the day of her glorious Annunciation. The first was virginity and purity so perfect that nothing can be compared to it amongst the purest creatures. Secondly, a most profound humility, united with a most ardent charity.

Although the angelic virtue of perfect chastity belongs more particularly to Angels than to men, nevertheless, Our Lady infinitely surpassed all the Angels in this virtue, because it possessed three great excellences not conceded to the Angels.

The first is that in Mary it is fruitful, whilst in the Angels it is sterile. The virginity of Mary is not only fruitful in having produced and borne the sweet fruit of life, our Blessed Saviour, but it is fruitful also because it produces a multitude of virgins, for (as we observed in the preceding consideration) if so many young persons dedicate and consecrate their purity to God, it is that they may follow her example. But the pure virginity of

Mary not only possesses the property of being fruitful, it can also restore virginal purity in those souls who have defiled this virtue by the contrary vice. In her lifetime she had already called many virgins to follow her, who became her inseparable companions; among others, St. Martha and St. Marcella. But it was also through her means that St. Mary Magdalen, who had been the scandal of Jerusalem, was enrolled after her conversion under the standard of virginal purity, and became like a brilliant crystal vase, capable of receiving and containing the most precious waters of grace.

The virginity of Our Lady, therefore, is not sterile, like that of the Angels, but it is so fruitful that from the moment she vowed it to God, until the present time, it has always borne its fruit. A soul that is perfectly dedicated to the service of God is never alone; many others, drawn by the sweetness of its perfumes, flock after to copy its example. It is on this account that the Spouse says to her Beloved: *Trahe me post te, curremus—'Draw me and we shall run.'*

Secondly, the virginity and chastity of the Blessed Virgin surpassed that of the Angels in this, that they are chaste by nature; and we do not, properly speaking, praise a person for the gifts of nature, since praise is not due where there is no merit. But the virginity of the Most Holy Virgin is, on the contrary, worthy of praise, because it was chosen and preferred by her, and consecrated by her to God. Although she was united in marriage to St. Joseph, it was without any prejudice to her virginity, because he to whom she was espoused had also consecrated his virginity to God.

Thirdly, the virginity of Our Lady surpassed that of the Angels, because it was subjected to the severest trials, whilst that of the Angels could never be tempted or tried. In this sense St. Augustine, addressing the Angels, says: 'It is not difficult for you, O blessed spirits! to be pure and remain virgins, because you neither are, nor can be, tempted.'

Some may, perhaps, wonder that I have said that the purity of Our Lady was exposed to the severest trials; and yet so it was. But we must not suppose that these trials were similar to our own. As she was all purity, these assaults could not be like our own. The temptations which come to us, who, unhappily, bear their incentives within our hearts, could never have ventured to approach that wall of her virginal integrity. But was it not a great trial for Our Lady when the Angel appeared to her in human form? And did she not manifest this in the fear and perturbation which assailed her, so that the Angel was obliged to reassure her in these words: *Ne timeas, Maria—'Fear not, Mary'?* By them he wished to remove the disquiet which her virginal purity suffered; it was as if he were to say: You see me in human form, but I am no man, nor do I come to you on the part of any man.

Modesty, says a holy Doctor, is, as it were, the sacristan of chastity. The sacristan of a church keeps an eye always to the altars, that nothing may be stolen, and he fastens the door with care. In like manner virginal souls are jealous to preserve this virtue unspotted, and no sooner do they perceive danger, or even the shadow of danger, than they are quickly alarmed. Thus it was with the Most Blessed Virgin, who was not only the Virgin *par excellence* of all in heaven and on earth, but also the most humble of all, and she manifested in this mystery of the Annunciation, the most sublime act of humility that a pure creature could make. When she heard herself called by the Angel *full of grace*, and received the announcement that she should become the Mother of a Son Who was to be both God and Man, she was troubled, and filled with fear; because, although she had conversed familiarly with the Angels, she had never heard them utter a single word in her praise.

The Most Holy Virgin would here teach us the dangers to which purity is exposed by the desire of praise. Humility is the inseparable and necessary companion of virginity, which could not long be maintained in a soul that was not humble. It is true that in persons who live in the world one of these virtues may subsist without the other, as we see in the married life, but in regard to virgins, it must be absolutely asserted that one who does not profess both these virtues has neither of them except in appearance.

Our Lady, being reassured by the Angel, and having understood what her Lord had decreed to work within her, made a sublime act of humility, saying: *Ecce ancilla Domini, fiat mihi secundum verbum tuum—'Behold the handmaid of the Lord, be it done unto me according to Thy word.'* It was thus she expressed herself at the very moment when she saw herself raised to the sublimest dignity that can be imagined. An incomparable dignity, indeed, is that of Mother of God, but it does not disturb the humility of Mary. Although she is raised above all creatures, nevertheless she simply declares that she is, and ever will be, the servant of His Divine Majesty; and to show the truth of her protest she adds: *Fiat mihi secundum verbum tuum:* 'Be it done unto me according to Thy word.' She abandons herself to the Divine Will, and proclaims that of her own choice she would never have come forth from her state of humility and lowly self-esteem. How well did the Most Holy Virgin know that humility is ever the inseparable and necessary companion of virginity!

Although, as we have said, humility and virginity can dwell singly in persons who live in the world, yet such a separation can never be made between humility and charity, these virtues being absolutely inseparable. They are like the ladder of Jacob, by which the Angels ascended and descended. This was not done simultaneously, but alternately; the Angels descending first, and then ascending afterwards. Similarly, as soon as humility has abased us, charity quickly raises us up towards heaven. It might seem that the virtue of humility in some degree removes us from God, Who is at the summit of this mysterious ladder, because it causes us to descend very low in self-abasement. On the contrary, however, in proportion as we lower ourselves we become more and more worthy to mount towards the summit of this mystical ladder of perfection, where our Heavenly Father awaits us. Our Lady, then, obtained the dignity of Mother of God by abasing herself, and acknowledging herself unworthy of it; for scarcely had she protested her lowliness, and abandoned herself, by an act of incomparable charity, to the Divine Will, than the mystery was accomplished. If we thus regulate our conduct, and, in imitation of Mary, unite virginity with humility, we shall be certainly helped by charity. This Divine gift will lift us up the mystical ladder of Jacob, and introduce us into the presence of the Eternal Father, Who will enrich us with every kind of heavenly consolation. We shall sing canticles of Divine praise with our most holy Patroness, and eternally glorify Our Lord for the grace we have obtained to imitate her virtues, and fight under her standard.

SPIRITUAL FLOWERS

Humility made the Son of God descend from Heaven into the immaculate bosom of Mary, and by the same virtue we may also cause Him to descend into our souls.—*St. Teresa.*

It is not humility to acknowledge ourselves to be miserable, for this needs but a little understanding of our condition, but to *wish* and *desire* to be treated as such is true Christian humility.—*St. Francis de Sales.*

We ought never to make use of our heart, eyes, and words for the indulgence of our own humours and inclinations, but only for the service of the Celestial Spouse.—*The same.*

EXAMPLE

The Love of St. Alphonsus for Mary

The love of St. Alphonsus Liguori for the Blessed Virgin Mary was so burning that he desired to inflame with it the hearts of all mankind. He was often heard to say: 'O men, what are you doing? Why so much affection for earthly creatures, for false deceivers, who make you lose both body and soul, both Paradise and God? How is it you love not Mary, who is ever most amiable, most loving, and most faithful; and who, after having enriched you with consolations and graces in this life, will obtain for you from her Divine Son the eternal glory of Paradise?'

He loved her so tenderly from his childhood, that one day he said to her quite simply: 'O my sweet Virgin Mary, I do not wish that there should be anyone in the world who loves and hononrs you more than I do;' and this desire of his heart was fully gratified. He thought of her even in sleep, and made use of this tender aspiration: 'O Mary, how beautiful you are! O how beautiful you are!' No one could speak to him without receiving a recommendation to be devout to Mary. 'Be devout to the Holy Virgin Mary,' he would say; 'whoever is devout to her will certainly be saved.' He inculcated the pious practices of visiting her images, reciting the Rosary, and fasting in her honour, on Saturdays and on the vigils of her festivals. But in a special manner he wished all to recite, every morning and evening, three *Ave Marias* in commemoration of her Immaculate Conception and perpetual virginity, adding this aspiration to each Ave Maria: 'By your sacred virginity and Immaculate Conception, O Mary, obtain for me purity and sanctity of soul and body.' He gave pictures of her to everyone, saying: 'Here is the image of your Heavenly Mother; give her your love and confidence.' At other times he repeated: 'Love the good Virgin much, because Mary is the Mother of perseverance; and whoever loves Jesus and Mary will become holy.'

Prayer.—O Mary! you are truly the valiant woman in whom the Lord found rest, and whom He has chosen to be the depositary of all His treasures. The universe honours you as the most pure sanctuary of the Divinity, the true Temple of the Lord, in which was begun the salvation of the world, and in which took place the grand reconciliation between God and man. You are that privileged field which sin could not enter and devastate; you are that magnificent garden in which Our Lord planted all the flowers that adorn His Church. You, O Mary, are the Paradise of God, whence springs the fountain of living water which waters and fructifies the earth: obtain for me, by your powerful intercession, that, being washed in this most pure water, I may be admitted with you to the nuptials of the Immaculate Lamb. Amen.

Aspiration.—Most pure Virgin, pray for us.

Practice.—In temptations against holy purity invoke Mary, Virgin and Mother.

Eighth Day

The Visitation

Though Mary had thus humbled herself before God, she did not stop there, because she knew that humility and charity do not attain their highest degree of perfection until, for God's sake, they are exercised in behalf of our neighbour. True fraternal charity proceeds from the love of God, and in proportion as this increases, the love of our neighbour becomes more intense. The Apostle of Charity teaches us this truth, when he says: *Qui enim non diliget fratrem suum quem vidit, Deum quem non videt, quomodo potest diligere?*—'For he that loveth not his brother whom he seeth, how can he love God whom he seeth not?' If we desire, then, to show our love to God, we must love our neighbour, we must serve him, help him, and relieve him in his necessities according to our power. How profoundly was the Blessed Virgin penetrated with this truth! No sooner had she heard that her cousin had conceived in her old age, than she arose and went with haste (the Gospel says, *cum festinatione*) over the mountains of Judea to the city of Ephrem.

Consider that Mary is become the Mother of the Son of God, and having with all humility and sweetness obtained leave of her Holy Spouse to go and visit her cousin Elizabeth, she bade a painful adieu to all her neighbours. With great eagerness did the Most Holy Virgin undertake her long and fatiguing journey, as the Gospel says, she *went with haste!* The first movements of Him Whom she bears in her womb increased her fervour, and she began her journey with haste but without mental flurry. The Angels are ready to accompany her, and St. Joseph gladly conducts her. One would wish to have known something of the conversation of these two great souls, and willingly should we listen to the account thereof. It is probable that the Holy Virgin conversed only of Him Whom she bore within her, and breathed only for her Saviour. St. Joseph, on his side, thinks only of his Redeemer, Who moves his heart with a thousand sentiments and affections. As wine locked up in the cellar acquires the scent of the flowery vines, so the heart of this Holy Patriarch insensibly participates in the perfume and the vigour of the Divine Infant Who blooms in His beautiful vineyard. The profound humility which Mary exercised in serving one who was in every respect her inferior, is indeed most worthy of our admiration. It is true that Elizabeth was of noble birth, because she was of the royal race of David, and was, moreover, united in marriage to the High Priest of the tribe of Levi. However, this nobility is nothing in comparison with that of the Most Holy Virgin, whose incomparable greatness can only be expressed by the title of Mother of God—*Mater Dei*—and yet where can we find more profound humility? Her humble heart is not satisfied with calling herself the handmaid of the Lord, but she leaves her house, and for three entire months is as a handmaid to her venerable cousin. The Gospel, moreover, gives us to understand that when the Divine Mother entered the house of Zacharias she was the first to give the salutation, and this through her great humility: *Intravit in domum Zachariæ et salutavit Elizabeth.*

Remark also the conduct of Our Lady amidst the praises and blessings which Elizabeth bestowed upon her. Assuredly it was very different from that of women in the world, who instead of humbling themselves when they are praised, become more puffed up. Was it not vanity that possessed our poor mother Eve, who, on hearing that she was created to the image and likeness of God, became thereby so presumptuous that she strove to become equal to Him, and gave ear to all the suggestions of the infernal enemy? But as the Most Holy Virgin had come into the world to regain all that Eve had lost by her vanity and pride, she thinks only of the abyss of her nothingness, and calls herself the handmaid of the Lord, although proclaimed by the Angel His Mother; when she is declared by Elizabeth to be the most blessed of women, she replies that her blessings are accorded because the Lord has looked down upon her lowliness and her littleness: *Quia respexit humilitatem ancillæ suæ*. What an excellent sign is humility of heart in a soul that has made progress in the spiritual life! When such souls humble themselves before God and before all creatures, in proportion to the greatness of the favours received, and place all their happiness, like Mary, in this alone, that the Divine Goodness has looked down upon their lowliness and misery, it is a sure indication that the graces of God are not received in vain.

The effects of grace in the heart of the Most Blessed Virgin were a profound humility and a burning charity towards God and towards her neighbour. The Apostle St. Paul in relating to us the love that our Saviour bore to the virtue of humility, says that 'He humbled Himself unto death, even to the death of the Cross'—

Humiliavit semetipsum usque ad mortem, mortem autem crucis; and he would have us learn from this that we should not be satisfied to have practised this virtue in some particular circumstances, nor for a certain time, but that we must practise it always and on all occasions. We must practise this virtue not only *until death* but *unto the death of the Cross;* that is to say, unto the perfect mortification of ourselves, humbling our self-esteem and our self-love. Let us not deceive ourselves by a certain appearance of humility; as, for instance, in speaking of our imperfections, or in performing external acts of reverence and humility, for the virtue of humility does not consist in this. True and Christian humility makes us esteem ourselves absolutely as nothing, as unworthy to live, as deserving only of universal contempt. It moves us to embrace generously the precept of our Saviour, that we renounce ourselves if we wish to follow Him: *Si quis vult post me venire, abneget semetipsum.*

SPIRITUAL FLOWERS

Humility is the root of every virtue. As the flower receives its nourishment from the root, and withers when it is cut off from it, so virtue, however perfect it may be, languishes and dies if it be not rooted in humility.—*Nouet.*

Bees suck honey from the lily, the iris and the rose; but they draw it also from the smallest flowers, such as rosemary and thyme. Indeed, they gather more honey from the latter, and it is of a better quality; because more closely confined in the smaller flowers and better preserved. Thus is charity practised, both more frequently and with more humility, in lowly exercises of devotion, and consequently with greater perfection and holiness.—*Francis de Sales.*

EXAMPLE

The Pilgrimage of St. Francis de Sales to Loreto

St. Francis de Sales was always thinking of the honour of the Most Blessed Virgin, and had made a vow from his youth to visit the holy Chapel of Loreto. In his travels through Italy, made by order of his father, his great desire was to fulfil the promise he had made to venerate the Most Holy Virgin in the Sanctuary where she had received the visit of the Angel and the sublime dignity of becoming the Mother of God, and he did so with wonderful piety. He was rapt in admiration in beholding those walls that had enclosed such wonders. He prayed motionless for a long time before the Altar of the Queen of Heaven, thanking her devoutly for all she had done for himself, exhorting her to continue her holy protection, and renewing his promise to imitate her angelic virtue of purity during his whole life. Ineffable were the graces and consolations that he then received; his mind was illumined by celestial light, and his heart was inflamed with such ardent charity, that from that moment nothing appeared to him impossible, when there was question of the glory of God and the salvation of souls.

Prayer of St. Germanus.—Hail Mary! you are the hope of Christians, and it is in this quality that I turn myself to you. Receive, O tender Mother, the prayer addressed to you by a poor sinner, but a penitent sinner, who honours you, and who, after God, places in you all his hope for his conversion and salvation. I am indebted to you for so many graces, but grant me, I beseech you, one grace more. Confirm me and establish me in the grace and love of your Divine Son. You are the consolation of the afflicted; deign, then, to intercede in my favour with your Divine Son, my Saviour, Jesus, that He may deliver me from the burden of my sins, dissipate the darkness of my understanding, remove every irregular affection from my heart, and restrain all the efforts and temptations of my enemies, that, being aided by this grace, I may henceforth so order my life that, under your protection, I may arrive at the happy port of eternal life. Amen.

Aspiration.—O Holy Virgin! may I always remember you, and have recourse to you in all my necessities.

Practice.—Visit the altar of Mary, either in the church or in your room, to obtain from her sorrow for your sins.

Ninth Day

The Charity of Mary in the Visitation

We must not imagine that the Blessed Virgin Mary was moved to undertake this long journey to visit her cousin, St. Elizabeth, by curiosity to know if what the Angel had told her were true, for she had not the slightest doubt of it. Our Blessed Lady was moved by a secret impulse of God, Who wished to commence the work of Redemption and the sanctification of souls in this visit, by the sanctification of the infant St. John.

The most ardent charity and most profound humility animated her, and gave her wings to fly across the mountains of Judea, and these two virtues were also the cause of her journey. As St. Ambrose says, charity or grace knows no delays nor cold deliberations: *Nescit tarda molimina sancti spiritus gratiæ*. It need not therefore surprise us if the Most Holy Virgin, filled as she was with charity (because she bore in her womb Him Who is Love itself), should exercise it in continual acts towards God, to Whom she was closely united by the sacred bond of perfect love, and towards her neighbours, whom she loved so tenderly and sincerely that she sighed for the salvation and sanctification of the whole world. She went with all alacrity, because she knew with what happy results her visit would be attended, in the person of St. John, and also because she wished to congratulate her cousin who, notwithstanding her age and sterility, had conceived the long-predicted precursor of the Word Incarnate. She went that they might rejoice together, and excite each other to glorify the God of all mercy, and to thank Him for so many favours and benedictions.

St. Luke would teach us by the words, *Exurgens Maria abiit cum festinatione in montana in civitatem Juda*—'Mary arose and went into the mountain country with haste, into a city of Judea'—the care and readiness with which we also ought to correspond to the Divine inspirations. As it is the work of the Holy Spirit to banish all tepidity and negligence from the heart, so He would have us execute His Divine Will with all care and diligence, and He is offended by any kind of delay. The virginal purity of Mary, which so dearly loved solitude, also caused her to go with haste, for the best protection for virginal purity is to appear as little as possible in the tumult of the world.

Having reached the house of Zachary, she entered it. She saluted Elizabeth. The Evangelist does not relate that she saluted Zachary also, for her love of purity was so great that she spoke little with men. Let virgins learn from this that they cannot take too great care for the preservation of this virtue.

Who can imagine the sweet fragrance of this most beautiful lily in the house of Zachary during the three months that she remained there? How well did she spend every instant! What honey, what precious balsam, must those sacred lips have distilled in the few but excellent words that they uttered! Indeed, Mary could speak only that which filled her heart, and *that* was Jesus!

Let us consider the meaning of the words, that 'Elizabeth was filled with the Holy Ghost'—*Et repleta est Spiritu Sancto Elisabeth*—that Elizabeth, who had already received the Holy Ghost with all His gifts, received a new fulness and a new increase of grace by this visit. Although the Lord grants His graces to the just *in full measure*, yet, as the Gospel says, this measure can be so augmented as to overflow on all sides: *Mensuram bonam confertam et coagitatam et supereffluentem dabunt in sinum vestrum.*

Let us well understand this important truth. The grace of the Holy Ghost can never be granted to us in this life in such full measure that it cannot be augmented; therefore, let us beware of saying: 'It is enough; I am sufficiently enriched with graces and virtues. *Mensura conferta est*—the measure is filled up, further progress in mortification is unnecessary.' He who should speak thus would only show too clearly his misery, or, rather, his presumption, and the great danger to which he exposes himself. *Omni habenti dabitur et abundabit, ei autem qui non habet et quod videtur habere auferetur ab eo*. This text signifies that to him who has received much—that is to say, who has laboured much, and never gives up—much shall be given. Such a one believes that he has never done enough; but, conscious of his own misery, he continues to labour with holy and sincere humility. *He, then, who possesses much, shall receive with usury, and superabundantly;* but from him who profits not by the grace received, letting it lie idle and fruitless, because he believes he is rich enough, *from him shall be taken that which he thinketh himself to possess and that which he does not possess*. This means, that graces already received shall be taken away, because he has not traded with them, and those which have been prepared for him shall not be bestowed upon him, since he has rendered himself unworthy of them by his negligence. All this, however, is not to be understood of *sufficient* grace, which is never denied by God to anyone, but of *efficacious* grace, which, by a just judgment of God, is not granted to tepid and ungrateful souls.

The thirst for riches and honours, by which worldlings are tormented, never allows them to say, *Enough*. And yet they ought to be contented with a little, for experience teaches us that the highest dignities and honours and great wealth frequently occasion the loss of souls. It is in regard of such temporal matters that we should say, *I have sufficient*. But, with regard to spiritual goods, let us never believe that we possess them in sufficient abundance, so long as we remain in this land of exile, but let us make every possible effort *to advance day by day from virtue to virtue*.

Experience teaches us that plants and fruits do not attain maturity until they have produced their seeds, which are necessary for the reproduction of their species. In the same way our virtues will never be sufficiently perfected, or reach their maturity, until they produce within us an ardent desire to make further progress. This desire is the spiritual seed which produces new degrees of virtue.

SPIRITUAL FLOWERS

Mary is a most beautiful rose, which dared not open its petals even to the gentle breeze of an Angel!—*St. Ambrose.*

How precious and how delicate a flower is purity! A sigh, a look, a word is enough to wither it! On this account chaste souls continually distrust themselves, and flee from the slightest occasions of danger.—*Nouet.*

The rose is the symbol of love and charity; its petals are red, and formed like a heart. Such should be the actions of the spouses of Jesus Christ. They should have as many hearts as they have petals—that is to say, hearts full of love, and like petals in the little esteem they should have of their actions.—*St. Francis de Sales.*

EXAMPLE

Consecration of the Saturday to Mary

Holy Church is ever desirous to maintain a tender devotion in the hearts of the faithful towards the Most Blessed Virgin, and from the earliest ages of Christianity she has encouraged the consecration of the Saturday to her. It is related that there was in the church of

Santa Sofia at Constantinople a picture of the Mother of God which was veiled during the rest of the week, but on Friday evening the veil was raised without human aid, and lowered on the evening of Saturday. Thus did Almighty God manifest His Will that *Saturday* should be dedicated to Mary. It was on Saturday she took so great a part in the work of our redemption, and it was fitting that on the morrow of the day when she so bitterly wept over the sorrowful scene of Calvary we should remember her tears shed for us in a special manner. Again, on Saturday God rested from His work in the creation of the world, and the Church consecrates this day to her, to honour the mysterious repose of the Holy Ghost in her Immaculate Heart, and that of Our Blessed Saviour in her chaste womb. Saturday is the introduction to Sunday—the symbol of eternal rest—and the Holy Virgin is truly invoked under the title of 'Gate of Heaven'—*Janua Cœli*.

Saturday, moreover, is the day between Friday, the day of mourning, and Sunday, the day of joy—and the Holy Virgin is the mediatrix between God, Who is Eternal Beatitude, and man, who is subject to endless evils and miseries. Mary is the way to arrive at Jesus, and Saturday is a prelude to the solemnity of Sunday. Saturday is as a magnificent portal consecrated to the

Mother of God, by which we enter the Sanctuary of God Himself. The Saints held this day in great esteem—on it they redoubled their pious exercises—and many begged, as a signal favour, that they might die on a Saturday.

Prayer.—O Sovereign Queen of Angels! you are the Mother of Orphans, as your faithful servant, St. Bonaventure, says: *Mater Orphanorum*. Sinners are truly orphans—for they have had the misfortune to lose their God, the most tender of Fathers. To you, therefore, I have recourse, O Mother of Mercy. I have had the misfortune to lose my true Father, by sin; and yet, since you have not abandoned me, O my Mother, I feel a lively hope that through your goodness you will deign to intercede for me, and reconcile me to my Father, Whom I have so grievously offended. O Holy Virgin! he alone can perish who does not have recourse to you. I confess, indeed, that I am a most unworthy sinner, and, nevertheless, to you do I fly, animated by sweet confidence in your love. Your mercy is greater than all my miseries; and, although my iniquities are enormous, they will never exhaust the treasures of your Son's mercy, nor your own. I sincerely detest, from my heart, all my sins, and hope, through your intercession, for a general pardon. Amen.

Aspiration.—O Mother of God and my Mother, the confidence I place in you is to me a pledge of my eternal salvation.

Practice.—Let all your prayers and actions this day be offered in suffrage for the holy souls in Purgatory.

Tenth Day

By the Visit of Mary, Elizabeth Is Filled with the Holy Ghost

Let us continue our Meditation on the sweet mystery of the Visitation.

The visit which this incomparable Virgin made to St. Elizabeth was not useless, nor, like the visits of worldly people, a matter of ceremony. Such visits result in harm to the conscience, in offences against chastity or charity. The Most Holy Virgin was induced to visit her cousin Elizabeth from pure motives of charity, and the days she spent with her were not employed in useless occupations, but in praising and magnifying God. How holy, pious, and devout was not this visit! It filled the whole house of Zachary with the Holy Spirit, and admirable effects were produced in St. Elizabeth. The first effect was humility. As soon as Our Lady appeared in the house of her cousin the Saint was filled with astonishment at such a favour, and exclaimed: *Unde hoc mihi ut veniat Mater Domini mei ad me?*—'Whence is this to me, that the Mother of my God should come unto me?' This is the virtue that the Holy Ghost first produces within us; a profound humility, which forces us to annihilate ourselves in the sight of the infinite greatness of God, and acknowledge our own baseness and worthlessness.

The second effect was to confirm St. Elizabeth in faith, as is gathered from the words she ad dressed to the Most Holy Virgin: 'Blessed art thou that hast believed; blessed art thou among women, and blessed is the fruit of thy womb'—*Beata es quæ crededisti; benedicta tu inter mulieres, et benedictus fructus ventris tui*. Indeed, one of the chief operations of the Holy Spirit is to ground us in faith and convert us entirely to God, and make us acknowledge Him as the Source of all the graces and blessings granted to mortal beings.

Truly may St. Elizabeth have said, you are blessed amongst all women, but your blessedness proceeds from the Fruit of your womb, the God of blessings. We do not usually praise the fruit on account of the tree, but the tree on account of the excellence of its fruit. Thus, although we ought to render to the Most Holy Virgin a worship or veneration beyond that which we render to the Saints, yet our homage and veneration should never equal that which we give to God. God alone should be sovereignly adored; but, as the Most

Holy Virgin is the Mother of Our Saviour, and a co-operator in our redemption, she is worthy of such a special worship as all true Christians have ever given to her. When the Holy Spirit dwells within us, we love and praise God alone above all things, as our Sovereign Creator; and after Him, Mary, His Most Holy Mother.

The third effect that the Holy Ghost produces in those upon whom He descends is a complete change of heart, as is represented in the joy of the Baptist yet unborn: *Ecce enim ut facta est vox salutationis tuæ in auribus meis, exultavit infans in utero meo*—'Behold, as soon as the voice of thy salutation sounded in my ears,' said Elizabeth to Our Lady, 'the Infant leaped in my womb.' Thus was St. John sanctified, going forth as it were out of himself, and casting himself before his Maker. And so it is with those who receive the Holy Spirit: they go out of themselves and lose themselves in God; that is to say, they live no longer according to nature and the senses, but they follow the inspirations of grace. If you desire, then, to know whether you have received the Holy Ghost, examine your actions.

It was through the intervention of Most Holy Mary that St. Elizabeth received the Holy Spirit. This teaches us that we should make use of her as a mediatrix with her Divine Son in order to obtain heavenly graces. It is true that we can address ourselves directly to God in our petitions, without employing the mediation of the Most Holy Virgin or the Saints; but this is not according to the order ordained by God, Who wished that there should be a communication between us and His Saints. Hence the Church militant and triumphant form but one Church, directed and governed equally, though differently, by God Himself; and He wishes us to have recourse to Him through the Most Holy Virgin and the Saints, and He bestows the most precious graces upon us by their intercession.

For the concluding point of this meditation we may add that it is of the greatest advantage to our souls to be visited by the Most Blessed Virgin; and her visits are always accompanied by many blessings and graces, as in the case of St. Elizabeth. O God! you will say, I do, indeed, desire that she would deign to honour me with one of her visits during prayer, since her visits fill the soul with sweet consolation. However, we must bear in mind that Mary often visits us with inspirations and interior lights, to aid our progress in perfection; and these are precisely the visits that we are unwilling to receive.

Endeavour to receive Holy Communion devoutly, and you will contract a spiritual relationship with the

Most Holy Virgin, since the Most Precious Body of Our Saviour, which we receive in Holy Communion, was formed by the Holy Ghost of her most pure blood.

In this manner, and by the imitation of her virtues, the relationship which you will contract with her will be much more excellent and more pleasing to her than that of Elizabeth, which was merely of flesh and blood. Our Lord says: 'Whosoever shall do the will of My Father Who is in heaven, he is My brother, and sister, and mother' (Matt. xii. 50).

In order to have some share in the visits of this Holy Virgin, we must not look for consolations, but generously resolve to accept even contempt and sorrow. In fact, Mary did not visit St. Elizabeth until she had suffered the ignominy and humiliation of her sterility. It is impossible to lead a devout life without trouble, and merit is in proportion to suffering. Finally, if we desire to receive the favour of this visitation, we must be transformed; we must die to self, and live only to God and for God: in a word, we must humble ourselves profoundly, according to the example of St. Elizabeth. Be faithful then, pious souls, in this exercise, during this short and miserable life, that you may afterwards chant eternally in heaven with the Most Holy Virgin:

Magnificat anima mea Dominum!—'My soul doth magnify the Lord!'

My God! how ashamed I am to be still so full of myself, when I have so often come to Holy Communion! O dear Jesus! may we always bear Thee in our hearts, that we may no longer breathe but Thee? How is it that I am so little united to Thee, since Thou art always in me? Why do I stray so far from Thee, whilst Thou art always close to me? Thou dwellest in my heart, how is it that I do not abide in Thine?

SPIRITUAL FLOWERS

Chastity is the unblemished beauty of the Saints, which, like the rose, adorns the soul and body, and fills them with sweet and pleasing fragrance.—*St. Ephrem.*

A slight breath of wind suffices to make the flowers fall from the trees in spring; and sometimes one flattering word, of itself, is enough to ruin a chaste soul, which is infinitely more delicate and tender than any flower.—*Nouet.*

As the bee gathers from flowers the dew of heaven and the sweetest juice of the earth, forming it into honey and carrying it to its hive, so the Priest takes from the altar our Blessed Saviour (the true Son of God, Who descended like dew from heaven, and came forth from the Virgin Mary as a flower from the earth of our humanity), and places Him in your mouth, and He becomes to you a delicious and spiritual food.—*St. Francis de Sales.*

EXAMPLE

Devotion of St. Thomas Aquinas to the 'Ave Maria'

The most tender devotion towards Mary was, as we may say, innate in St. Thomas Aquinas. One day, when he was a little child, his nurse observed that he kept a piece of paper in his hands, which she wished to take from him: but the child resisted with loud cries, and made every effort to retain it. This singular resistance excited the curiosity of his pious mother, the Countess Theodora. She therefore took hold of the piece of paper, opened it, and found, to her surprise, written upon it the Angelical Salutation. Whilst she was reading it, the infant redoubled his cries and tears, so that she was obliged to return it to him. Thomas had no sooner received it, than putting it into his mouth he swallowed it with great eagerness. This fact foreshadowed the devotion which the Saint ever had for the Angelical Salutation, on which he has left us a most pious and learned commentary, full of the praises of Mary.

Prayer.—Holy Virgin and my tender Mother! You are the channel by which the graces of God reach us; you are the depositary of all celestial treasures, and you yourself declare to us that you possess all the wealth of heaven, to enrich those that love you: *ut ditem diligentes me*. O Divine Mother! you see that my poverty is great, and my indigence extreme; but remember, I beseech you, that I trust in you, and hope that you will be moved to compassionate my miseries, and to obtain for me a remedy. I love you, O Holy Virgin; you are, after God, the great object of my affections. Have compassion on me then, and never abandon me to the snares of the enemies of my salvation, but succour me during the whole course of my life, and above all at the moment of my death, so that I may come one day to your feet, in the abode of eternal happiness. Amen.

Aspiration.—O Holy Virgin, help those who groan in misery!

Practice.—Mortify self-love, by some act of obedience or meekness.

Eleventh Day

Humility of Mary

The Blessed Virgin Mary surpassed all the Angels and Saints in perfection and merit; and of all creatures none as she was so pleasing to God. Who, indeed, ever possessed so ardent a charity and so profound a humility? Where shall we find humility equal to that which appeared in Mary when, in answer to Elizabeth, she confessed that the cause of her happiness was that the Lord had deigned to regard the humility of His handmaid, and that therefore all generations should call her blessed?—*Quia respexit humilitatem anciliæ suæ; ecce enim ex hoc beatam me dicent omnes generations.*

Many Doctors of the Church are of opinion that, when Mary said, 'the Lord hath regarded the humility of His handmaid,' it was not her intention to speak of her virtue of humility, because, although she was profoundly humble, she did not believe herself to be so; but that she thought only of her lowly state, her baseness, and abjection as a creature of God, and of the nothingness from which she had been drawn.

There are others, however, who hold a contrary, and perhaps more probable, opinion, and say that Our Lady intended to speak of her virtue of humility, being well aware that it was this virtue that had attracted Our Saviour to her chaste womb. We may well believe that Mary was aware that she possessed this virtue, and that she had no fear of losing it, being intimately persuaded that it was the effect of the grace of God within her and not of her own merits.

Indeed, we find the great St. Paul acknowledging that he possessed the virtue of charity, and in such decisive terms as would seem in others presumptuous rather than humble. He writes: 'Who shall separate me from the charity of Christ?'—*Quis me separabit a charitate Christi?* 'Shall tribulation, or distress, or hunger, or nakedness, or danger, or persecution, or the sword? I am sure that neither death nor life nor Angels shall be able to separate us from the love of God, which is in Christ Jesus our Lord.' See Rom. viii. 35-39.

Notice the confidence with which this great Apostle speaks when he protests that there is no power in the world, or in hell, that is capable of separating him from the charity of his God. He believed that he possessed this virtue of charity; and in speaking thus he confided entirely in grace, and in his own merits *by grace*. The glorious Virgin knew well that the virtue of humility has more power to attract the Heart of God to our hearts than all other virtues. The Divine Spouse in the Canticles seems to signify this, when he expresses his admiration for the beauty of the footsteps of his beloved: *Quam pulchri sunt gressus tui in calceamentis, filia principis!*—'How beautiful are thy steps in shoes, O Prince's daughter!' (Cant, vii. 1), and then enumerates her other beauties. Judith did not captivate Holofernes so much by the rare beauty of her countenance and the splendour of her attire as by her sandals, or her shoes, which were probably embroidered with gold.

In like manner the Eternal Father, considering the variety of virtues that adorned Our Lady, was in admiration of her beauty; but when He cast His eyes upon her sandals He was so pleased that He sent His Only Son to become Incarnate in her chaste womb. What is signified by these sandals or shoes of Mary but her humility? These articles are the least valuable part of our attire, and the soonest covered with dust. Now, the spirit of true humility continually abases the souls who possess it, and annihilates them in their own eyes, and keeps them under the feet of everyone. Such is the property of this virtue of humility, which is the foundation of the whole spiritual life. It was this lowliness that the Lord looked upon in the Most Holy Virgin with so much complacency, and this look of His formed her whole greatness: *Quia respexit humilitatem ancillæ suæ, ecce enim ex hoc beatam me dicent omnes generations*. All generations shall call her blessed *because* God had regarded her.

Whichever of the two significations given to these words: God hath regarded *the humility of His Handmaid* be accepted, we find that the Holy Virgin always spoke with so much humility as to leave no doubt whatever that she considered all her happiness to proceed from her Lord having looked upon her lowliness. On this account the words of the Spouse of the Canticles are applied to her: *Dum esset Rex in accubitu suo nardus mea dedit odorem suum*—'While the King was at his repose, my spikenard sent forth the odour thereof.' The plant on which the spikenard grows does not grow up high like the cedars of Lebanon. But lowly as it is, it delights all by the sweetness it diffuses around. What a precious plant was the Most Holy Virgin, who never sought to exalt herself, although enriched by God with the most signal favours! She was always penetrated by the sense of her own abjection and nothingness; and in virtue of this humility she spread around, like the spikenard plant, so sweet a perfume that it ascended to the Throne of the Divine Majesty, and attracted the Son of God to descend and take flesh in her immaculate womb.

We see, then, how dear humility is to God! Our Saviour taught this truth in His memorable reply to the woman who exclaimed aloud: *Beatus venter qui Te portavit et ubera quæ suxisti*—'Blessed is the womb that bore Thee, and the paps that gave Thee suck.' 'Yea,' said Our Lord, 'rather, blessed are they that hear the Word of God and keep it'—*Quinimmo beati qui audiunt verbum Dei et custodiunt illud*. That is to say: 'My Mother is indeed blessed on account of having borne Me in her womb; but more blessed is she on account of the humility with which she listened to the words of My Heavenly Father, and kept them.' And this He again taught when He said that they who heard the Word of God and practised it were to Him as His Mother and His Brethren.

SPIRITUAL FLOWERS

Jesus Christ built His throne upon the ruins of the world. Before the fruits of grace can be gathered the flowers of prosperity must fall.

The present moment's grace may be that which will decide our eternity.—*Nepveu.*

The Heart of Mary is a garden of delights, in which we can gather the most precious fruits. This most beautiful garden is closed against the impure spirit; it is full of Divine perfumes, cultivated by a Heavenly Hand, and adorned with the most charming flowers of virtue. Of these there are three which particularly attract our admiration, and fill the house of God with the sweetest fragrance—they are the violet of humility, the lily of chastity, and the rose of charity.—*St. Bernard.*

The less you seek after praise and your own interests, the more do you deserve to be praised and rewarded by God.

EXAMPLE

Origin of the Rosary

The Rosary of the Blessed Virgin Mary in its present form was instituted by St. Dominic. But as early as the year 1094 Peter the Hermit had invented a kind of rosary of beads of wood, upon which the Crusaders, who were generally uneducated men, recited a certain number of *Paters* and *Aves*, varied according to the solemnity of the feasts.

Historians also relate that even before that time pious persons were in the habit of reciting a series of *Paters* and *Aves* upon knotted cords. In the East it was the custom to present crowns of roses to persons of distinction. St. Gregory Nazianzen, moved by ardent piety towards the Mother of Our Redeemer, offered to her, instead of a material crown of roses, a spiritual crown of prayers. It consisted of a long string of the highest praises and most glorious titles and excellent prerogatives of Mary.

St. Bridget, Patroness of Ireland, who lived in the fifth century, developed this pious idea of St. Gregory by substituting for those prayers which were unknown to the people the more popular and more beautiful prayers of the *Credo*, the *Pater*, and the *Ave Maria*. And to regulate the number of prayers to be recited, the Saint adopted the method of the anchorets of threading beads of stone or of wood together in the form of a crown or chaplet.

The word 'Rosary' signifies a crown of roses, and the prayers, the expression of the heart's affections, of which it is composed, are spiritual roses with which we adorn the head of our dear Blessed Mother.

It is said that a holy solitary was watching one day a poor old woman reciting her rosary with great devotion, when he observed an Angel by her side holding a golden thread, upon which he strung a rose for every *Ave*, and a lily for every *Pater*; afterwards he placed this garland in the form of a crown upon the head of the old woman, and disappeared, leaving behind him a sweet fragrance of roses. This fragrance was often perceived in former days in churches, after the recital of the Rosary.

Prayer.—O Mary, my good Mother! obtain for me an ardent love for your Divine Son, my Saviour Jesus Christ. From Him you can obtain all that you desire; obtain, then, for me the grace to be always so united to the Divine Will that I may never again be separated from it. I ask you not, my Mother, for earthly goods, nor honours, nor riches; but I ask of you that which you have much more at heart, the grace to love my God. Is it possible that you should refuse to assist me in a work which is so agreeable to you? No; you will help me, my good Mother—you will pray for me. Pray then, O Sacred Virgin, and cease not to pray for me, until you see me in heaven, out of danger of losing my God, and certain of loving Him throughout eternity. May I be able to thank Him for ever, with you, my good and charitable Mother, for so great a mercy. Amen.

Aspiration.—Make me like unto you, O Mary, who were so sweet and humble of heart.

Practice.—Make an act of external humility in union with Mary.

Twelfth Day

Through the Blessed Virgin Mary, St. John the Baptist Receives the Most Special Graces

Who could number all the graces and favours showered upon the house of Zachary, when the Holy Virgin entered it? If Abraham received many graces for the hospitality he gave to three Angels; if Jacob was the cause of so many blessings to Laban, an idolater, in whose house he dwelt; if Lot was saved from the fire of Sodom, for having given shelter to two Angels; if the Prophet Elias filled with oil all the vessels of the poor widow who entertained him; if Eliseus raised to life the son of the Sunamitess his hostess; if Obededom obtained so many favours from Heaven, for receiving into his house the Ark of the Covenant—how great and precious must have been the graces and blessings poured upon the house of Zachary for having lodged for three months the Angel of the great Council, the Divine Prophet, the real Ark of the Covenant, Our Lord Jesus Christ inclosed in the immaculate womb of Mary! Who could understand the

Divine sweetness poured into the heart of Elizabeth during the time of that Divine visitation? How profound must have been her meditation on the mystery of the Incarnation, and what thanks must she have offered to God for all the favours bestowed upon her. But, above all, very special favours were conferred by Our Lord upon His precursor St. John Baptist.

Firstly, according to the common opinion of the Fathers, St. John received the use of reason; secondly, from that moment he was sanctified; and thirdly, he was filled with the knowledge of God and of His Divine mysteries. Even then he loved his Saviour, he adored Him, and leaped for joy in His presence, as we learn from Elizabeth herself, in the words she addressed to the Holy Virgin: *Ecce enim ut facta est vox salutationis tuæ in auribus meis, exultavit infans in gaudio in utero meo*—'Behold, as soon as the voice of the Salutation sounded in my ears, the Infant in my womb leaped for joy.'

Such extraordinary joy was not surprising. Jesus Christ, speaking to the Jews, says: *Abraham frater vester, exultavit ut videret diem Meum*—'Abraham, your father, rejoiced to see My day.' All the prophets desired ardently the promised Messiah, and rejoiced that at His coming their predictions would be fulfilled.

We may well believe, therefore, that St. John rejoiced at the presence of this long-desired Messiah, in the immaculate womb of the Holy Virgin, Who had come to visit him and begin the work of Redemption, delivering him from original sin. It would not have been fitting that he, who was chosen to prepare the way of the Lord, should, at his birth, bear the stain of original sin. On this account, therefore, Our Lady repaired to the house of St. Elizabeth, that the Child, Whom she bore and Who was the Sanctifier of souls, might, in this visit, purify the glorious St. John from original sin and sanctify him. This He did with such fulness of grace that many Doctors are of opinion that he never sinned even venially. The charity, of which the heart of our glorious Queen was full, caused her to co-operate in this work of sanctification. No wonder that she should have been so ardent in love and zeal for the salvation of men when she bore in her bosom Charity Itself, the Saviour and Redeemer of the world! All faithful souls should rejoice when they are visited by our Divine Saviour in the Most Holy Sacrament of the Altar, or by the interior graces which are so often vouchsafed them, or by the many inspirations and loving words which He addresses to them when knocking at the door of their hearts. Under what an obligation are they not to correspond to so many favours, and with what care and fidelity should they not fulfil the Most Holy Will of their Divine Saviour!

O my dear Sisters, Daughters of the Visitation of Our Lady and of St. Elizabeth, since you have Mary for your Mother, you should have nothing so much at heart as to imitate her particularly in her humility and charity. These are the two virtues which especially animated her when she visited the house of Zachary. Like her, you should visit, diligently and joyfully, your Sisters, when they are suffering, and endeavour to aid each other in your spiritual and temporal infirmities. Be most careful and diligent in those things in which humility and charity are most required. To be numbered amongst the Daughters of Our Lady, it is not sufficient to live in a house of the Visitation and wear the Religious habit. If you would not wrong such a Mother, you must imitate her in her virtues and the sanctity of her life. Be careful, then, to conform your life to hers. Be mild, sweet, humble, charitable, good; magnify Our Lord continually with her, and be assured, beloved souls, that, if you fulfil your duties with humility and fidelity during the whole course of your life, you will, after death, be admitted to the

Holy Virgin in heaven, singing, '*Magnificat anima mea Dominum.*'[3]

SPIRITUAL FLOWERS

A soul dedicated to God entirely, in act and in will, deserves that God should give Himself entirely to her.—*St. John of the Cross.*

We ought always to have our eye fixed upon the Will of God alone, recognising it, and with all joy, or at least courage, following it carefully in all our actions. But even this is not enough; we should also love this Will of God, whatever it may cost us.—*St. Francis de Sales.*

---

3 As soon as the Most Humble Virgin heard herself praised by St. Elizabeth, she humbled herself, and referred all the glory to God in that most beautiful and admirable canticle of the *Magnificat*, which far surpasses the canticles by the women of the old Law. It is far more excellent than that of Judith; more beautiful than that of the Sister of Moses, after the passage of the Red Sea; more sublime than that of Deborah and Baruch, after the victory gained over the enemies of the Hebrew people. The canticles of Zachary and of Simeon, with all those of the Old Testament, cannot be put in comparison with this Divine Canticle.

It is a highly valuable exercise of piety, to follow always the Will of God, instead of our own natural humours and inclinations.—*The same.*

EXAMPLE

Conversion of the Celebrated Pianist, Hermann Cohenn

The compassionate mercy of the Most Holy Virgin has at times been admirably displayed in behalf of the Sons of Israel. To the name of the Abbé Ratisbonne, so well known to the servants of Mary, we must add that of another Jew, converted by the Mother of Divine Grace.

Hermann Cohenn, a German by birth, and a Jew in religion, had acquired great fame in Paris as a pianist and composer of music. He says of himself: 'I was courted and applauded in society, and as I possessed understanding beyond my years, I soon had instilled into me all the fearful doctrines that the powers of hell have taught in the earthly hell of Paris. Atheism, pantheism, socialism, licentiousness of manners, etc., all found a place in me, so that I had become one of the most zealous propagandists, and therefore a great favourite of all the new prophets of hell. . . .'

Whilst this second Saul was thinking out ingenious projects for the perversion of innocent hearts, he was requested by the Prince of Moscow to take the direction, during his absence, of a choir of singers who were going to sing the praises of the Blessed Virgin Mary at a church in Paris during the month of May of 1847. Although he was a Jew, still he consented; and it was there, before the Altar of Mary, that grace awaited him. Whilst he was rendering external honour to the august Mother of God, she pleaded his cause before her Divine Son. His moment of grace and benediction came at the very moment when he was looking with scorn and derision upon the piety of the faithful. . . Suddenly he feels an invisible weight upon his shoulders, which forces him, in spite of the obstinate resistance of his will, to bow his head and bend his knees; his mind is quickly illuminated by the light of Faith, and he feels his heart opening to the salutary impressions of grace. It would take too long to narrate the many obstacles which hell opposed to his conversion, but at last he triumphed over all, and on the Feast of St. Augustine, he was washed in the waters of Baptism, with the most heart-felt emotion; and upon the Feast of the Nativity of Mary, had the ineffable consolation of making his first Communion, and of receiving the Scapular.

Some time afterwards, finding himself called to Religion, he retired into a community of Marist Fathers, that he might there meditate seriously on his vocation; and finally, by the counsel of his Director, he chose to enter the austere Order of Carmel.

Having visited Rome and obtained the necessary dispensation, he was afterwards ordained Priest, and consecrated himself entirely to the glory and honour of Jesus and Mary.

He employed his great musical talent for the honour of the Queen of Angels. In order that all Christian tongues might bless the mercy of that Divine Mother, who had delivered him so wonderfully from the darkness of error, he composed *a collection of hymns for the month of May, and for the principal festivals of the year,* set to music for the organ or pianoforte.

The following extract from the dedication of these compositions will show his tender devotion to the Blessed Virgin: 'Morning Star! you appeared to me in the obscure night, in which I was lost! Health of the sick, you cured the mortal wounds of my heart! Refuge of sinners, you opened to me an asylum in your Immaculate Heart! . . .'

Glory then to Mary, and to the sweet and salutary devotion of the month of May, which procured us a new brother in Christ, and a new masterpiece of the grace of God and of the mercy of Mary!

Prayer (from St. Augustine and St. Bernard).—Remember, O most compassionate Virgin Mary! that it was never heard in any age that anyone who implored your protection has been abandoned by you. Animated by this confidence, I have recourse to you, O Mother of God, Virgin of virgins. Do not despise my prayers, Mother of the Divine Word, but graciously hear and answer me.

O Mother of God! you pray for all, and above all, for sinners; deign, then, to pray for me, a more obstinate sinner than any other, and therefore a more worthy object of your pity! You see plainly the urgent need I have of your intercession; therefore interest yourself in my regard, and obtain for me, from your Divine Son, the grace of sincere conversion and holy perseverance. Amen.

Aspiration.—I place myself for the whole of my life under your protection, O Mother of my God! O show that you are my true Mother!

Practice.—Be very attentive in all your exercises of piety during the day.

Thirteenth Day

The Trials and Consolations of the Blessed Virgin

We can never meditate too much upon the great and cruel sorrows with which the heart of the august Virgin Mary was afflicted during the whole course of her life; yet she was the most holy of creatures, the most beloved by God. 'You,' exclaims St. Chrysostom, 'who bitterly weep and lament, under the contradictions and afflictions that assail you, are you not ashamed to desire and seek for such a happiness as even the Holy Family did not enjoy? Ponder, I beg of you, the vicissitudes and changes to which they were exposed!'

Mary receives the glad tidings that, by the operation of the Holy Ghost, she should conceive a Son, the Lord and Saviour of the world. What a joy to her heart is this! and what rapturous delight filled her soul at the moment of the Incarnation of the Word in her most chaste womb! But this celestial joy is quickly followed by sorrow. Her Spouse, St. Joseph, is alarmed at the prodigy, and thinks of secretly abandoning her. Oh! the affliction of Mary when she sees the perplexity of St. Joseph, whom, through her humility and modesty, she is unable to comfort. After this most excruciating trial, the Angel discloses the celestial secret to her Spouse, and orders him to remain with her. What consolation fills the heart of these two Angelic Spouses at this announcement! But God had prepared new afflictions for them. They must abandon their happy retirement, and journey to Bethlehem in obedience to the order of the Emperor Augustus. Faithful souls, lose not sight of Mary in this mystery; remain near this Mother, and abandon her not for an instant, whilst she journeys from Nazareth to Bethlehem. Without any painful solicitude, but with most ardent desires, she awaits the birth of the Blessed Fruit of her immaculate womb. You will see this beautiful Lady, the fortunate Daughter of Sion, beg hospitality, and not find a shelter in the whole of Bethlehem, although she is the Mother of the King of Glory. However, she blushes not for her poverty and misery, but considers it rather an honour to have to endure it.

Many holy affections are awakened in our hearts by this Divine birth; but we are especially taught the spirit of perfect detachment from all worldly pomps and worldly gratifications.

It seems as if there were no mystery that so much unites tenderness with austerity, love with rigour, bitterness with sweetness, as this mystery of the Nativity. Where can we find a poorer, and yet a more illustrious birth, or a Mother so blessed? She who gives birth to the Son of God has certainly no need of the consolations of the world!

Let us then delight to dwell near the sacred manger, where the Saviour of our souls so powerfully speaks to us in His silence and teaches us so many virtues; and let the joy and consolation of the Son and of the Mother form all the happiness of our souls! How well it becomes Mary to caress this Infant! How enchanting her charity in allowing all who wish it to look at Him, to touch and embrace Him! Do you also ask her to give Him to you, and she will do so.

O my Jesus! what a sweet night is this! The Church sings that the heavens everywhere distil honey. It would seem that those blessed Angels, who make the air resound with their song, gather this celestial honey from the breast of the sweet Virgin Mary, and from her chaste Spouse St. Joseph.

What is there that we can give to our little King that we have not received from His Divine abundance? Let us, then, give Him our hearts, which He prizes above all. O Saviour of our souls, transform our hearts into gold, through charity; into myrrh, through mortification; into incense, by prayer; and then receive us within the arms of Thy Divine Protection, and let us hear Thee say, from Thy Sacred Heart, 'I am thy Salvation for ages of ages.'

SPIRITUAL FLOWERS

'A bundle of myrrh is my Beloved to me. He shall abide between my breasts' (*Cant.* i. 12), in order that I may incessantly inhale its bitterness.

The afflictions of this life are like the flowers that precede the fruits of glory; and the blood which we shed is as a royal unction which consecrates us to immortality.—*St. Greg. Nyssen.*

The rose grows amidst thorns; and the most beautiful and most solid virtues grow amidst the severest contradictions.—*St. Francis de Sales.*

No one will be crowned with roses, if he be not first crowned with the thorns of Our Saviour.—*The same.*

Our actions are like roses, which, though more pleasing when fresh, are yet sweeter and more agreeable when faded. Thus, although works performed with consolation are more pleasing to us; yet if they be done in the state of aridity, they have a sweeter odour, higher value before God.—*The same.*

EXAMPLE

A Fortunate Mistake

The following is related by an eye-witness of the event: 'One evening, in December, 1855, a Priest named B——, having returned to his house after a hard day's work, sat down and began to recite his Office, when he heard a knock at his door. He opened it, and saw a young girl, who asked him to go and visit a dying lady, living at No. 28, — Street. . . . The good Priest was ready to interrupt his prayer to follow the little messenger, but she told him there was no hurry, provided he went in the course of that evening; so he wrote down the address of the sick person, and told her to say that he was coming shortly.

'After finishing his Office, the good Priest went to the street named, and entered No. 18, thinking this was the number mentioned. It was a wretched house, and as there was no one in charge of the door he walked in, groped up the poor staircase, and knocked at the first door that he came to. A man opened it, and at the sight of the ecclesiastical dress, fell into a passion, and to the inquiry made as to whether this were the house of the sick lady, he made an impudent answer, and shut the door in the face of the Priest. Patient and mild, like his Divine Master, the Priest knocked at the next door, and met with no better reception. He then went up to the second story, where he found a boy playing in a passage. "Can you tell me, my child," said he, "where I can find a poor lady dangerously ill, who lives in this house, and is called G—?" "Yes; down there, Reverend Sir; my father said that she would not be able to live through the night; but I do not think that you have said her name correctly." "Never mind the name; lead me, I beg of you, to her door."

'The Priest, preceded by the child, entered the room and found a woman in her agony; a man about fifty was sitting near her bed, and at the sight of the Priest he immediately arose, evidently annoyed. "Are you Mr. G?—" said the Priest; "how is your sick wife?" "No," replied the man bluntly, "I am not; who has sent you here to meddle with other people's affairs?" "I was requested to come," replied the Priest with surprise. "I was told that a poor lady, named G—, was seriously ill, and wished for the last consolations of religion. I may have mistaken the street, or the house, or room; but undoubtedly this sick woman has much need of my ministry. The Divine Mercy has certainly led me here, and allowed this mistake to occur." "Yes, man of God!" murmured the dying woman, "yes, it is God Who has led you hither." "Nothing of the sort," said the husband angrily; "for ten years no Priest has set his foot in my house; you shall not confess my wife. I am her master; mind your own business." "You are much mistaken, sir," answered the Priest, firmly and mildly; "the first Master of your wife is God, and you have no right over her soul. If she desire, I shall hear her confession, and I can only withdraw when she freely and of her own will refuses my ministry." Then, approaching the sick woman, he said: "Madam, do you desire to be reconciled with God, and die a Christian death?" The poor woman raised her hands to heaven, and shed tears of joy, exclaiming: "Blessed be the Divine Goodness that has allowed this mistake! for three days I have been asking my husband for a Priest, and he has answered me only with insults. I do truly wish to be reconciled to my God, Who has had so much compassion on my poor soul." "Do you hear, sir?" said the Priest to the husband; "be pleased to leave me alone with her for a few moments." These words, pronounced with much firmness and resolution, forced the man to retire, although he did so grumbling.

'The dying woman then pointed to a rosary hanging over her bed, and said: "See, this has saved me; I had the weakness to fear my husband more than God, and to avoid disturbances and quarrels, for ten years I have given up every practice of religion. One only thing have I preserved—the love of the Most Holy Virgin, and confidence in her intercession. I have recited her Rosary almost every day; it is she alone who has led you here, and she, the true Mother of Mercy and refuge of sinners, saves my soul." The Priest was deeply moved by this touching narrative. He consoled the sick woman, helped her to make her confession, and then told her to prepare to receive the Holy Viaticum and Extreme Unction, whilst he went to give notice thereof to the Parish Priest.

'On leaving the house he looked at the address which the little girl had given him, and saw that the number was not 18 but 28. Blessing God for this fortunate misunderstanding he hastened to No. 28, where he found the sick lady expecting him. After complying with the duties of his sacred ministry here also he immediately went to the Parish Priest to see about the other Sacraments which the two sick persons required; but meanwhile, the poor woman at No. 18 died. She had received the pardon of her sins by the sacramental absolution, and the fervour of her will would assuredly supply before the God of All Mercies for the other succours of religion.

'The man of God, full of faith and gratitude towards the Most Holy Virgin—the refuge of sinners and consolation of the afflicted—then proceeded to fulfil the duties of his sacred ministry towards the other dying lady.'

This most touching fact shows once again the treasures of benediction that result from piety towards the Most Blessed Virgin, and the great Mercy of Our Adorable Saviour towards those who love His Holy Mother.

Prayer of St. Bernard.—O Mother of Mercy! even when on earth you were deserving of our veneration and confidence; but now that you are raised to the highest heavens your faithful servants look to you as the help of all nations. We beseech you, then, All Holy Virgin, to succour us by your patronage and prayers. Your prayers are more dear to us and more valuable than all the treasures of earth; they are so efficacious that they obtain from God the abundance of His graces; so powerful that they suppress and bring to naught all the efforts of our enemies, who labour for our destruction. Scatter them, O Mother of Mercy! confound all their designs, strengthen our weakness against their malice, and show yourself the true Mother of all the faithful who place their confidence in you. You are all my hope, and will be so as long as I have breath. Amen.

Aspiration.—I place all my confidence, after God, in you, O Mary, my dear Mother.

Practice.—Bear patiently, and in a spirit of penance, all the contradictions you may meet with this day.

Fourteenth Day

Mary at Bethlehem

God resolved to confer on mankind the most signal and loving benefit of the Incarnation, and came down upon earth into the desert of this world like a celestial manna, that He might become our food, during our journey to the promised land of Paradise. Our adorable Saviour rendered Himself visible to us at His birth, as a beautiful little Infant, lying in a manger, and this was in the night, when the world was covered with darkness. The Divine Nature of Our Lord Jesus Christ is represented by the honey contained in the manna—because honey is a celestial liquor gathered by the bees from flowers, and it is not distilled from their sap, but collected by them as it descends from heaven with the dew. In like manner the Divine Nature of our adorable Redeemer came down from Heaven, at the moment of the Incarnation, upon this blessed flower of the earth, the Most Holy Virgin, and, having become united with a human nature, preserved it in the bosom of the Most Chaste Mary, as a sweet hive, during the space of nine months.

But let us consider more at length this miracle of Divine Mercy.

The Most Holy Mother of God gave birth to her Divine Son as the stars produce their light; and on this account her name Mary truly signifies Star of the Sea, or Morning Star. The star of the sea is the Polar star, towards which the mariner's needle continually turns; and through this star those who navigate the ocean know how their course is directed.

The Patriarchs, Prophets, and Fathers of the Church turned their eyes towards the Most Holy Virgin, and she was ever the Polar Star and the chosen Port for all poor mortals who navigate the sea of this miserable world, and by her means they may avoid those shipwrecks which occur so often on the rocks and precipices of sin.

Mary was, also, that beautiful Morning Star which brought the joyful news of the coming of the Sun of Justice. The Prophets knew well that a Virgin would conceive and give birth to a Son, at once God and Man, through the operation of the Holy Ghost, and would still remain a Virgin, though she became a Mother: *Ecce Virgo concipiet et pariet Filium et vocabitur ejus Emanuel.* How should He Who selected her for His Mother, on account of her virginity, impair her integrity? How could the Eternal Word, Purity itself, lessen the virginal purity of His Mother? From eternity He is generated and virginally produced in the bosom of His Father; and although receiving from Him the Divinity, it is not divided, but the Word is always one and the same God with the Father. The Most Holy Virgin here on earth also produces virginally her Divine Son, Our Lord. There is this difference, however, that He will never again enter the bosom of Mary, but He will be eternally generated in the bosom of His Father, being One with Him, in virtue of the unity of the Divine Essence.

This Divine generation may indeed be made the foundation of our meditations on the mystery of Our Lord's Nativity; but it does not admit of a curious inspection, nor should we weary our mind by endeavouring to examine into that which is too sublime for our weak understanding: *Generationem ejus quis enarrabit?*—'Who shall declare His generation?' says the Prophet Isaiah.

But now, after having considered the virginal purity of the Most Holy Virgin in giving birth to her Divine Son, let us turn our eyes to this Divine Infant, and see how He allows Himself to be cared for by His Holy Mother, as if He could not do otherwise. Why is this? It is to teach us how to act, Religious especially, who are bound by the sweet chains of the holy vow of Obedience. Our Lord certainly could not make bad use of His Will, or of His liberty, being the Eternal Wisdom; nevertheless He concealed His knowledge, and all His perfections as God and those of His perfect human intellect, under the swathing bands of infancy. He keeps hidden under the veil of holy obedience to the Eternal Father, Who had willed that He should be, as St. Paul says, in all things like to His brethren, excepting sin. Behold our Model! Let us often visit this Child, lying in a manger; and let us learn from Him how to act in all things according to His Most Holy Will.

But shall we visit Him empty-handed? The shepherds took with them some of their little lambs to present to Him. What can we offer more acceptable to this Divine Pastor of our souls than our hearts as a little offering of our love and the choicest part of our spiritual flock? How dear will this offering be to Him! He will look upon us with mercy in return for our gift; and we shall gladden the Most Holy Virgin, who so much desires our welfare. Let us take with us from her Divine Infant one of His precious tears, the sweet dew of Heaven, and place it on our heart, that it may henceforth feel no other sorrow than that which rejoices this Blessed Infant—that is, sorrow for sin! We should all be like so many simple shepherds watching over the flocks of our affections, ready to adore this our Infant Saviour, as soon as the Angels call us. We should offer Him, as a pledge of our eternal service, the finest lamb we possess; that is, all our love, without any reserve or exception.

Oh, how happy shall we be, and what great consolation shall we receive, if we thus visit the Saviour of our souls!

As the manna had the taste of every kind of food, so this Divine Infant contains in Himself every kind of consolation. Each one can find in Him what he desires, and proportionate to his capacity, provided that he possess the requisite dispositions.

SPIRITUAL FLOWERS

No flower could be a better emblem of the resplendent virtue of Mary and her singular privilege than the lily; whose three petals may signify that she was a Virgin in her conception of Jesus, a Virgin at His birth, and a Virgin ever afterwards.—*Nouet.*

Mary is the Mystical Lily without spot, in which the Eternal Word espoused our nature.—*The same.*

The flower falls from the tree when the fruit is formed; but the Mother of God, who is the tree of life, preserves her flower and her fruit, and by an unheard-of miracle unites maternity to virginity.—*The same.*

As the lily lifts its stem on high, so the soul who often receives Jesus Christ should direct its hopes towards heaven in imitation of Jesus, Who is the Flower of the field and the Lily of the valley. The virtue of such a soul has roots deeper than the cedars of Lebanon, which defy the winds and the storms. In the fruitfulness of her good works and in her charity towards the poor, her glory is like that of the olive. The fragrance of her holy life and of her sweet conversation is spread around like the odour of the flowers which bud forth on Mount Lebanon in spring-time.—*St. Cyril.*

EXAMPLE

The Devotion of the Saints to the Angelus

1. St. Alfonso di Liguori omitted no favourable opportunity for showing his tender devotion to

the Most Blessed Virgin. Whenever he heard the clock strike, whatever might be his occupation or conversation, he interrupted it to recite the Angelical salutation, saying that one *Ave Maria* was more valuable than the entire world. He was most exact in the recital of the *Angelus*. As soon as he heard the sound of the bell, he went down on his knees, even when he happened to be in the public streets. When he became deaf he desired to be warned of the ringing of the bell, and even when at his meals he would break off and kneel down to recite it. Often was he rapt in ecstasy during this prayer from the fervour of his devotion.

2. St. Charles Borromeo, who was so celebrated for piety and learning, was not ashamed, when Archbishop of Milan, to descend from his carriage or his horse in the open streets to recite the *Angelus* in honour of Mary.

3. St. Vincent de Paul, wherever he might be, or in whatever society, even at court, would recollect himself, and kneel down as soon as he heard the sound of the Angelus. He considered himself happy to be able to give public testimony of his filial love

of the Most Holy Virgin Mary, and those who were present always followed his example.

All who devoutly recite the *Angelus* on their knees morning, noon, and evening at the ringing of the bell gain a hundred days' Indulgence each time, and if they continue to say it at least once a day during the course of a month, they may gain a Plenary Indulgence on the usual conditions. Those who are unable to hear the sound of the bell may gain the same Indulgence by reciting the *Angelus* at the time that it is usually rung. As to those who are much engaged, and who wish to supplicate the Blessed Virgin thrice a day, they can supply for the *Angelus* the following invocations: Virgin before the birth of your Divine Son, pray for us; Virgin at His birth, pray for us; Virgin after His birth, pray for us. Lastly, those who do not know the prayers can say the *Paters* and *Aves* in memory of the Incarnation of the Word in the womb of Mary.

Prayer of St. Anselm.—We beseech you, O Queen of Heaven and Sovereign of the Universe, by the grace which Our Lord conferred upon you in raising you to so sublime a degree of glory, to intercede for us, that the fulness of grace with which you were enriched may render us one day partakers of your glory and happiness. O Mother, full of mercy, interest yourself in our behalf, that we may be able to enjoy the ineffable happiness for which our God deigned to inclose Himself for nine months in your most holy womb. If you deign to pray for us to your Divine Son, you will be assuredly heard. Let the bowels of your maternal mercy speak in our favour. If you, our tender Mother, have no compassion for us, what will become of your most miserable children? What will be our destiny when your Divine Son, as Judge of the living and the dead, will call us to His judgment-seat? Have pity on us then, O Mother of Mercy! Amen.

Aspiration.—See, O Mary, the many dangers by which we are surrounded, and have pity on our miserable condition.

Practice.—Let all your actions be done this day for the sole end of pleasing God, that you may thus be able to offer Him the tender lamb of your love.

Fifteenth Day

The Union of Charity and Humility in the Heart of Mary at the Incarnation

God is One; hence He loves unity and union, and hates all that is not in accordance with this unity. The reason is this—that as He is perfect in all His attributes, He must have a sovereign love for all that is perfect, and unity is perfection. He must also be averse to all disunion, because whatever is disunited is so far imperfect.

As then God wished to show us how dear to Him is union, He effected three distinct modes of union in the Most Holy Virgin on the day of His Incarnation.

Firstly, He united the Divine to the human nature; and so admirable and sublime is this union, that it infinitely surpasses all that human or angelic intelligence can comprehend. Nor could the Seraphim or Cherubim have ever imagined anything so wonderful. Indeed, two opposite extremes were to meet—the Divine Nature, which is essential perfection, and human nature, the deepest misery: the contraries being the greatest that can be conceived. Nevertheless, God in His Wisdom and infinite Goodness was able to find a method of uniting the two natures so intimately through His Incarnation in the womb of Our Lady that in one Person man was made God and God became Man, without disparagement to His Deity.

The second union was that of Maternity with Virginity. This certainly is most admirable and beyond all the laws of nature. A virgin becomes a mother, and remains still a virgin after maternity. This miraculous and supernatural union could only be effected by the omnipotent hand of God, Who granted this privilege to Mary; and as this union has been effected in her alone, so she alone will be eternally both a Virgin and a Mother, and the Mother of a Son Who is both God and Man.

The third union accomplished by God in our glorious Lady was that of the most ardent charity with the most profound humility.

Reflect on these two virtues, and you will ask how it is possible that charity can be united with humility, if the nature of one is to soar on high, and that of the other to abase itself? Naturally, indeed, it is impossible but God, Who is One, and Who loves and desires unity, manifested the greatness of His power by uniting these two dissimilar virtues in the soul of Mary.

In her, charity was so united to humility that one depended on the other, and whilst her charity continues humble, her humility is ever full of charity. Charity raised her soul above all creatures, and humility abased it below them all, and yet the union of these two virtues was continuous.

To what a high degree of humility and charity did not the Most Holy Virgin attain at the moment of the Incarnation! Ponder her words to the Archangel: *Ecce ancilla Domini, fiat mihi secundum verbum tuum*—'Behold the handmaid of the Lord, be it done unto me according to Thy word.' No sooner did she hear herself proclaimed the Mother of God, the Queen of Angels and of men, than she abased herself beneath all, saying: 'Behold the handmaid of the Lord!' This is a great act of humility.

The Most Holy Virgin in that moment had so clear a knowledge of the misery and nothingness of human nature, and of the infinite distance between God and man, that, seeing herself raised above all creatures, she abased herself beneath them all, considering her own nothingness and the infinite greatness of God Who had chosen her for His Mother. True it is, then, that

Mary never humbled herself so profoundly as when she pronounced these words: *Ecce ancilla Domini*—'Behold the handmaid of the Lord!'

But see how the Most Blessed Virgin united the most perfect charity to her humility when consenting to the proposal the Angel made her in the Name of God: *Fiat mihi secundum verbum*—'Be it done unto me according to Thy word'—were her words; and thus, by charity, she was raised above the Cherubim and Seraphim, and at that very moment the Eternal Son of God took flesh in her virginal womb, and she became His Mother!

Let us learn from the example of Our Lady that humility does not merely consist in diffidence in ourselves, but it must be accompanied by confidence in God. This confidence in God is produced by this diffidence in ourselves and in our own powers. This confidence is also the source of generosity of soul, of which Our Blessed Lady gives an example on this occasion when she says the words: 'Be it done unto me according to Thy word.' It is true, would she say, that I am unworthy of this grace, in regard to what I am only in myself; but as all that is good in me is from God, and as that which you announce to me is His Most

Holy Will, I believe that it can and will be done, and, therefore, let it be accomplished in me!

Humility conceals the virtues of a soul, in order the better to preserve them; nevertheless, when charity requires, it allows them to be known for their increase and perfection. Thus it resembles those plants which close their beautiful flowers at night and open them only when the sun is high, so that people speak of those flowers as sleeping during the night. Humility, in the same way, conceals all our virtues, and never allows them to appear, except for the exercise of charity, which, being a celestial, Divine gift, not an acquired virtue, is truly as a sun amidst all the virtues, and should always rule over them. Hence the humility, which is prejudicial to charity, is undoubtedly a false humility.

SPIRITUAL FLOWERS

Let us have a supreme contempt for all that is not God. Oh, how sweet it is to abandon one's self into His hands! Daily experience proves to us that the less we trust in our miserable efforts, the more does God work in us by His omnipotent virtue. All consists in being a docile instrument in His hands, and seemingly dead.—*P. Milley.*

It is good to leave Our Lord sometimes to serve others for His sake; and we should do so, if we can prevent our devotion from causing annoyance.—*St. Francis de Sales.*

As the olive, when planted in vineyards, communicates its savour to the vine, so charity communicates its perfection to the virtues amidst which it flourishes. It is also true that when the vine is engrafted on the olive, it not only receives its taste, but also its sap; thus we should not be satisfied with the possession of charity and with the exercise of all other virtues, but it is necessary that all our virtues be accompanied and produced by charity, and be attributed to this virtue alone.—*The same.*

EXAMPLE

The Efficacy of the 'Salve Regina'

The following appeared in the French journal, the *Univers:* 'We have already announced the departure of five Nuns of the Cross, on their way to apply their admirable spirit of unselfishness to the exercise of works of charity in the Diocese of Natchitoches, in America.

'After a painful misfortune at sea, these worthy Sisters have landed at Havre. They were to set out from this port, and in a letter addressed to the Bishop of Saint Brieux, the Mother Superior of the Sisters of the Cross thus writes:

"'Our Sisters started about eleven, on the morning of the 10th of November, 1856. They had received the blessing of our Chaplain, and did not expect ever to return; but Divine Providence had disposed otherwise. The steamer was already before Cherbourg, when, at about eleven o'clock in the night following their departure, a fearful noise was heard throughout the steamer. All the passengers were called to go on deck, and they came up exclaiming: 'We are lost! We are lost!'

"'One of the boilers had burst, and the explosion had wounded six men and set fire to the vessel. 'Have you a Priest on board?' said a lady to one of our Sisters. 'No,' she replied. 'So much the worse,' said the lady, 'because our death is certain.' 'No, madam,' calmly and confidently replied Sister Mary Agatha; 'let us invoke the Most Holy Virgin, and she will save us.' Our Sisters immediately went down on their knees, with their hands crossed on their breast, and recited the *Salve*

Regina. Many passengers and sailors joined them, and their cries reached the heart of the Mother of God. A few moments after, when the Sisters, who had gone down into a cabin, were continuing their prayers, they were informed that the fire had been miraculously extinguished, and that there was no further danger. No one doubted that their salvation was owing to the prayers which had been addressed to the Blessed Virgin Mary.'"—*Univers,* 30th November, 1856.

Prayer.—O most humble of Virgins, holy Mother of God, Mistress of life and Lady of the universe, teach me humility and the true love of this precious virtue. How great is the pride of my heart, who am but dust and ashes; I have eagerly sought for the praises of men, when shame and confusion for my innumerable infidelities should have made me feel my nothingness! Take pity on me, O Holy Virgin; banish the proud thoughts that arise in my soul, and let me imitate your humility here on earth, that I may be worthy to experience, with you, the truth of these words: 'The humble shall exult in the abundance of peace.' Amen.

Aspiration.—Pray for us, O most humble of all Virgins!

Practice.—Endeavour today to neglect no opportunity of practising humility and charity.

Sixteenth Day

The Purification of the Blessed Virgin

Let us meditate attentively upon the virtues of which Mary gives us so moving an example in the mystery of her Purification in the Temple. First of all, what more profound humility can be imagined than that practised by Our Saviour and Our Lady in their visit to the Temple? He comes to be offered, like all the sons of sinful men; she, to be purified like all other women. With regard to our adorable Redeemer, it is of Faith that He, being essential purity, could not be under the obligation of this Law, which was promulgated for sinners. With regard to the Most Holy Virgin, what need had she to purify herself, who, from the instant of her Immaculate Conception, had been endowed with purity so excellent, and with such a fulness of grace, that the highest Seraphim and Cherubim could not be compared to her? And yet, behold, the Son and the Mother, notwithstanding their incomparable purity, present themselves in the Temple, as if they were sinners like other children of Adam! O truly wonderful act of humility! If the value of this act increases in proportion to the dignity of the person who humbles himself, how full of useful instruction to souls tending to perfection is the humility practised by the Sovereign Creator of all things.

He shows us that this virtue was so dear to Him that He preferred death rather than relinquish its practice; for after teaching that there can be no greater love than to give one's life for the object beloved, He lays down His life for the exercise of humility. By submitting to die He, the immortal God, practised the most excellent and most sublime act of humility that can be conceived. Some persons deceive themselves by regarding humility as a virtue necessary merely to novices and beginners in the spiritual life, and the practice of which can be laid aside after some advance. But our adorable Saviour shows us how erroneous is this opinion, by humbling Himself unto death.

Oh if we could well understand the necessity of perseverance in this virtue! How many, after beginning well, have miserably fallen away because they did not persevere in the practice of humility! But Jesus Christ did not say he who *shall begin*, but he who *shall persevere* until death, shall be saved: *Qui perseveraverit usque in finem hic salvus erit.*

Genuine virtue may be distinguished from that which is only apparent, as true balsam is distinguished from false. Balsam is tested by dropping it into water; if it sinks to the bottom of the vessel it may be considered very pure and precious. We may know if a person be truly prudent, generous and noble, by observing if these virtues tend to make him humble, modest, submissive; for in such a case they are truly valuable gifts; but if they stay only on the surface, and love to show themselves and to win admiration, they are so far false and counterfeit.

The Angels, and, after them, our first parents, prevaricated through pride. Upon this account, Our Lord, like a wise and loving physician of our souls, applied the remedy to the root of the evil, and came into the world to plant in the place of pride the beautiful and useful virtue of Divine humility, become very necessary on account of the contrary vice being so general. Indeed, so common an evil is pride, that humility can never be sufficiently inculcated; and on this account, our adorable Saviour and our Immaculate Lady would obey the law, not made for them, to teach us to esteem this virtue. For us, who deserve only humiliation and contempt, to abase ourselves is no great thing. However, humiliation acquires an inestimable value when embraced by Jesus Christ and His Most Holy Mother; and this humiliation was continual with them throughout the whole course of their life. Wherefore the Apostle, speaking of the humility of Our Redeemer, said that 'He humbled Himself unto death, even to the death of the Cross'—*Humiliavit semitipsum usque ad mortem, mortem autem crucis*. But if we miserable creatures humble ourselves on some slight occasion, we quickly seek by every means in our power to indemnify ourselves for the transient exercise of this virtue, and the very thought of persevering in the practice of it alarms us. We are convinced, it is true, that we are very imperfect, and yet we desire to be looked upon as holy and perfect, notwithstanding the example of Mary, who consented to be clothed in the semblance of a sinner, although confirmed in grace and possessed of a more than angelic purity.

Observe any other daughter of Eve, and see how eagerly she seeks for honour and esteem; and although this defect be common to all mankind in general, it seems to be more marked in the female sex. Now, Our Lady and glorious Mistress is not the Daughter of Eve according to the spirit, but only according to the flesh, and therefore she always persevered in the most profound humility, and could say in her sacred

Canticle of the *Magnificat* that on this account 'All generations would call her blessed'—*Beatam me dicent omnes generationes*.

How beautiful is it to behold the Holy Virgin presenting herself and the Infant Jesus in the Temple, and making her offering of two doves! Happier is she than all the princes of earth! And what shall I say of the aged Simeon, who takes the Divine Infant in his arms? Let us also embrace Him, let us live and die in these tender embraces.

Place this sweet Jesus in your heart, like another Solomon upon his ivory throne. Let your soul follow His steps, that you may hear the holy words He continually breathes. Remember that your heart should be like ivory in purity and firmness; firm in its resolutions, and pure in its affections.

SPIRITUAL FLOWERS

Anything we do, however little, will have an inestimable value if it be done for the love of God.—*St. Teresa.*

It is an exalted degree of perfection to assimilate and conform ourselves to the spirit of the sacred Infancy of our most humble and most obedient Saviour.—*St. Francis de Sales.*

Whoever wishes to acquire virtue, and does not possess humility, is like to one who carries dust in his hands when there is a high wind.—*The same.*

EXAMPLE

Punishment of the Profaners of a Sanctuary of the Blessed Virgin

The holy Hermitage of Voiron did not escape the profanations of the heretics. They invaded it with arms in their hands, as if they were going to besiege a fortress; they ill-treated and expelled the Monks, took away the sacred vessels, the papers, documents, indulgences, etc., committed horrible sacrileges, and at last set fire to the place and entirely destroyed it, and rolled the remaining stones down the mountain.

This atrocious impiety was not left unpunished, for soon afterwards all who had taken part in the destruction of the hermitage perished miserably. It is remarkable, however, that in spite of all the devastation effected by these impious men, they could not gain their principal object, which was to carry off the statue of the Most Holy Virgin, which was preserved miraculously.

John Burgnard, a native of Chablais, who had embraced the heresy of the Bernese, and was the leader of these profaners, had no sooner reached the hermitage, than he mounted the Altar to carry away the statue of the Most Blessed Virgin. He threw a rope round its neck, and descending from the Altar was walking out of the Church, dragging the statue after him, and uttering at the same time these words: 'Come along with me, come along with me, little black woman' (the face of the statue was black); 'if you are as powerful as the Papists say, let me now have a proof of it. Why do you allow yourself to be thus shamefully dragged on the ground? Why do you not defend yourself?' He had no sooner uttered these blasphemies than the statue became immovable. The wretched man, finding that he was unable to drag it further, turned his head round to see what was hindering him, and by a second miracle his head remained turned in that direction, so that he could never again place it in its right position; and, moreover, he became crippled in an arm and a shoulder. Being obliged to leave the statue, he left the spot with great difficulty, and bore the chastisement of his impiety throughout his life, giving an undeniable proof of the sovereign power of the Queen of Heaven. But more terrible is the fact that he persevered in heresy, and died in despair in the presence of many of the parishioners of Bons. Amongst these were Michael Novello and Claude Ippolito Cortager, who gave testimony of this fact on oath A.D. 1629.

His Highness Duke Charles Emmanuel, when at Tortona during the time that St. Francis de Sales was converting the people of Chablais, verified the fact we have related, and ordered the secretary of the Town Corporation to register it, that the miracle might be transmitted to posterity. (See 'Life of St. Francis de Sales,' by Augustus de Sales.)

Prayer.—Holy Virgin! when you presented your Divine Son to the Eternal Father, you became dear to all the Heavenly Court. O present also our hearts, that, fortified by grace, we may never fall into mortal sin!

Most humble Virgin! when you placed the adorable Jesus in the arms of the aged Simeon, you filled his soul with, heavenly sweetness. O place our hearts in the hands of God, that He may fill them with His Divine Spirit! Most diligent Virgin, you co-operated in the redemption of the world, when you redeemed your Son Jesus with two turtle-doves; be pleased to redeem our hearts from the slavery of sin, that they may be always pure and holy before God. Most clement Virgin! when you heard from the lips of the holy Simeon the prophetic announcement of all your dolours, you submitted yourself quickly and perfectly to the Will of God. O help us to support always with patience and resignation all the tribulations of life!

Most merciful Virgin! bymeans of your Divine Son you illuminated the Prophetess Anna with supernatural light, so that she magnified the mercies of God and acknowledged and proclaimed Jesus as the Saviour of the world. O fill us with heavenly grace, that in the abundance of joy we may be able to reap the precious fruits of Redemption. Amen.

Aspiration.—O Mary! watch over me.

Practice.—Take every possible care today not to commit any sin, however venial it may seem.

Seventeenth Day

Mary, the Model of Perfect Obedience, in the Mystery of the Purification

Let us consider in this meditation how our adorable Saviour and His Most Holy Mother united perfect obedience to profound humility.

Our Lord preferred the death of the Cross rather than fail in obedience. 'Jesus Christ,' says the great Apostle, 'was obedient unto death, even to the death of the Cross'—*Factus obediens usque ad mortem, mortem autem crucis*. And what signal obedience did not Mary exercise at the death of her Son, the only object of her heart's affection! She stood firm and constant at the foot of the Cross, pierced with the sword of sorrow, perfectly resigned to the Will of the Eternal Father. All the actions of Our Divine Saviour were regulated by obedience, as He Himself declared, saying: 'I am come not to do My Will, but the Will of Him that sent Me'—*Descendi de cœlo non ut faciam voluntatem meam sed voluntatem ejus qui miset Me*. Thus He teaches us that the Will of His Heavenly Father was the sole guide of all His thoughts. Notice Our Lady's life, and you will always see her obedient. So highly did she esteem this virtue of obedience, that she obeyed the command to espouse St. Joseph, although she was bound by a vow of virginity. She always persevered in the practice of this virtue, and as the mystery of the Purification shows us, she presented herself in the Temple, that she might observe the Law she was not bound to observe. Thus her obedience was the more precious as it was voluntary. Indeed, this is the only virtue that she has recommended to the practice of mankind. The Gospel tells us that when she spoke to the attendants at the marriage of Cana, she said to them: 'Whatsoever He shall say to you, do'—*Quodcumque dixerit vobis facite*. Here she teaches the practice of holy obedience, which is inseparable from the virtue of humility, because it springs from this virtue. Only those who are truly humble subject themselves to the Will of God.

Our Lady had no fear of being disobedient, because she was not obliged to obey the Law, but she shunned its very shadow. Many would have misunderstood her conduct, if she had not gone to the Temple to offer her Divine Son and perform the ceremony of her Purification. She would, therefore, remove all suspicion of disobedience, and at the same time teach us not merely to avoid sin, but also its very appearance, and the occasions which may expose us to it. Let us learn, also, not to be satisfied with the testimony of our conscience alone, but to try to remove from others every occasion of thinking ill of us and of our actions.

The example of Our Saviour and of His Most Holy Mother should animate us to submit not only in those things that are commanded us, but in those that are merely of counsel, that we may thus become more dear to the Divine Goodness. O God! is it then so great a work to subject ourselves to obedience, when for this alone we have been sent into the world, and when the Supreme King, to Whom all things should be subject, practised it?

We must learn then from the example of our adorable Saviour and of His Most Holy Mother, to be docile, pliable, and easily ruled, not only for a certain time, and in some actions, but even unto death. But two fundamental conditions of this virtue of Obedience must be observed. These are—firstly, that to obey perfectly we must love God Who commands; and secondly, we must love the action that is commanded. All the faults committed against obedience proceed from the want of one of these conditions. Many love the thing commanded, but not God Who commands it. For instance, some will perform their devotions, not out of obedience to the Will of God, but on account of the consolation they experience in this exercise. In this there is nothing but self-love; and it will be perceptible by the repugnance, or discontent, which is felt in the performance of those observances that are not according to our inclinations. In this case, it is plain that it is not God Whom we love, but only the thing that He commands. If we loved God Who commands, our hearts would be indifferent as to our occupation, because in all we should be equally sure to find the Will of God.

Others will love God Who commands, but not the action commanded. These will say: I know very well that it is the Will of God that I should do this or that, but I feel so great a repugnance, that I cannot resolve to do it, and were I to strive to obey, the person who, in the name of God, desires me to perform the action, enjoins it so ungraciously, as to rob me of all the satisfaction I might experience in an act of obedience.

The source of all our difficulties is that we obey readily only when our superiors accommodate themselves to our natural inclinations. On all other occasions, the smallest obligations appear to us difficult and disagreeable. It is therefore evident that we do not regard God Who commands us through another, but we look at the person who speaks to us in His Name, to see how he is clothed so to speak; that is to say, we look only at his external deportment. O God! what a mistake! We ought to submit to the Will of God in obedience, without any exception, and from whatever quarter the order may come; and not only love God Who commands, but also the thing that is commanded; *taking the command and placing it upon our heads*—that is, in our inmost heart, to execute it with all fidelity and sincere goodwill.

SPIRITUAL FLOWERS

Bless God for having given you Mary as your Mother. Imitate her, and consider what a blessing it is for you to have so powerful an advocate in Heaven.—*St. Teresa.*

Humility cannot subsist without love, nor love without humility—and one can never be acquired without the other.—*The same.*

The more we mortify our natural inclinations, so much the more do we merit to receive supernatural inspirations.—*Francis de Sales.*

EXAMPLE

A Conquest of the Blessed Virgin's

Father Paul Stub, a Barnabite, became a conquest of grace, and an Angel in virtue and learning, through the intercession of the Blessed Virgin Mary. He himself thus relates his conversion in his excellent book for the Month of Mary, entitled 'The School of Mary':

'A Protestant youth set out from the North, in 1826, to take a post at Genoa, in the family of the Consul of Sweden and Norway, who was a very good Catholic. But the wife of the Consul, fearing that this youth might by his conversation have an evil influence on a nephew who lived with them, went to the sanctuary of Our Lady of Graces, and made the following prayer to the Queen of Heaven and Earth:

"'O Mary! if you see that this Protestant youth will become a Catholic and be virtuous, then let him arrive, but if otherwise, send his ship to America."

'The ship arrived safely at Genoa, and the boy entered on his situation. He was edified by the examples of virtue that he witnessed, but had no thoughts whatever of becoming a Catholic—until after some time, when he was in trouble, calling to mind the devotion which Catholics bear to Our Lady, he said to her: "O Mother of Jesus! it is the first time that I invoke you, but if you do me the favour I desire I will invoke you all my life."

'The favour was obtained most completely, and after that time the young man began to pray to God to know the truth, entered upon the study of religion, and became a Catholic in 1829, to his own great joy and that of many others. He afterwards took the Religious habit, and has since exercised his zeal for the glory of the Most Blessed Virgin in preaching; and, to give her a new proof of his gratitude, he composed this little book in her honour.'

Prayer.—Most pure Virgin! obtain for me the grace to understand henceforth the Divine sweetness of union with God. May my adorable Saviour abide with me under the veil of Faith as He dwelt with you in the seclusion of a hidden life! May He live in me through the union of my heart with His adorable Heart as He lived in you, forming one heart and soul with you! Oh that henceforth I may know how to love, to desire, and to relish only Jesus! May He alone, during the whole course of my life, be my strength, my life, the heart of my heart, the soul of my soul, that after having been frequently nourished with His virginal Body, which was conceived and born of you a Virgin, I may be able to say with the Apostle: '*I live now, not I, but Christ liveth in me.*' Amen.

Aspiration.—My heart is prepared to obey you in everything, O my Mother!

Practice.—Do everything you do today be done in the spirit of obedience.

Eighteenth Day

The Flight into Egypt.—Trust in Providence

The unspeakable joy which Mary and Joseph experienced after the birth of Jesus was of short duration.

The Angel of the Lord came again to visit Joseph in sleep, and said to him, 'Arise, and take the Child and His Mother and fly into Egypt, and be there until I shall tell thee, for it will come to pass that Herod will seek the Child to destroy Him.'

See how the heavenly messenger treats Mary and Joseph, precisely as if they were true Religious! How many pretexts might they not have found to be dispensed from obeying? Could we not wait till tomorrow? might they have said. What provisions have we for so long and tedious a journey? Who knows what we may have to suffer from the Egyptians, the declared enemies of the Israelites? Who will give us shelter in that country? These and a thousand other excuses would have been made by us had we been in their place. But perfect models as they were of submission and of confidence, they set out without delay, certain that God would provide for all their necessities. And so it proved, for they found lodging and food, either by means of the trade exercised by St. Joseph, or by the alms bestowed upon them.

That we may not lose even one of the many instructions given us in this touching mystery, let us consider first that Our Lord, the Eternal Wisdom, does not Himself take the charge of His Family. Being perfect God and perfect Man, He already possessed the use of reason, and from the first instant of His Conception He could have made known to Joseph and to His Blessed Mother all that was to happen to them. However, God the Father had conferred upon the Angel Gabriel the care of the Holy Family, and therefore Our Lord would take no part in it. The Angel commands and is obeyed most faithfully, although he was inferior to Jesus and also to Mary, who, as Mother of God, was endowed with greater graces and perfections than all the celestial spirits.

But this is not all. Observe the order that reigns in this Holy Family. Who can doubt that Our Lady was superior to St. Joseph in discretion, as well as in all the other qualities required for good government? And, nevertheless, the Angel does not inform her of all that is to be done, but he informs her Spouse, St. Joseph. It might appear strange that he addresses himself to him rather than to Mary, the Mistress of the house, who carries the Treasure of the Eternal Father. Had she not every reason to be offended at this proceeding of the Angel, who seemed thus to ignore her? She could undoubtedly have said to her Spouse, 'Why should I go into Egypt, when neither my Son nor the Angel have made it known to me?' But Our Lady is silent, and obeys with all simplicity, without being in the least concerned that the Angel had only spoken to St. Joseph. She knew well that all had been ordained by God; she does not even inquire the reason, but the knowledge that such is the Will of God is sufficient to secure her prompt submission. It is thus God acts towards men—to teach them holy and loving submission. A merely human mind does not wish to yield and to adore the secret mysteries of God and of His Most Holy Will until it is able to ascertain *the why and the wherefore of this and that*. A thousand reasons are brought forward as of greater discernment or experience, and so on; but they only cause disquiet, ill-temper, and complaints. From the time we begin to criticise everything disturbs us. Let us be satisfied to know what God wants of us, and let this suffice. But (some will say) who can assure us that such is the Will of God? This shows that our hearts would prefer that God should manifest everything directly to us by means of secret inspirations, or that He should send an Angel to announce to us His Will. And yet he did not thus reveal it even to Our Lady, but wished her to come to the knowledge of it through St. Joseph, to whom she was subject, as to her superior. Our self-love would like to be instructed sometimes by God Himself by means of ecstasies, visions, etc. We indulge ourselves in follies such as these that we may not be subject to the common and ordinary path of subjection to our rules and our superiors. Let it suffice for us to know that God wills our obedience without reflecting on the mental capacities of those who command us, and we shall accustom ourselves to walk with all simplicity in the happy road of holy and tranquil humility, which will render us pleasing to God. O! how many wonderful examples of obedience to the Will of God did not this glorious Virgin leave us during her whole life, and, above all, in her flight into Egypt! Whither, O glorious Virgin, do you direct your steps with that little Infant in your arms? I am going into Egypt, she replies. But why do you go there? Because it is the Will of God. For how long? As long as it pleases God. When will you return? When He shall command me to do so. But when you return will your heart be more happy than at present? O no, certainly not. And why? Because I fulfil the Will of God equally in going, in remaining there, and in returning. When you return, will you go into your own country? She replies, I know no country but the accomplishment of the Will of my God in everything.

O admirable example of obedience! Let us, in imitation of the Blessed Virgin, endeavour to submit to authority at all times and in every circumstance, whether it be pleasing to us or not. Let us go with all simplicity even as far as Egypt—that is, into the midst of enemies—because God Who sends us there will know how to protect us, and assuredly we shall not perish. On the contrary, if we remain in Israel with our enemy, self-will, it will certainly be the destruction of us. In imitation of Mary and Joseph, let us answer the suggestions of the enemy of our soul when he urges us to disobedience in these words: *Deus providebit*—'God will provide.' O my God! happy we if we could accustom ourselves to answer our heart always thus when it becomes anxious, and thus banish all solicitude and trouble. Great indeed is the confidence which God asks of us in His Paternal care and Providence; but why do we refuse it to Him when we know that no one has ever been deceived in Him, but, on the contrary, has always reaped therefrom the most copious fruits? And was not this the promise which Our Saviour made to His Apostles when He urged them to this loving confidence? 'Your Father in heaven knoweth that ye have need of these things.'

SPIRITUAL FLOWERS

Obedience has the property of changing the flower of our desires into the fruits of good works. Shun singularity as far as possible, and do not make yourselves different exteriorly in any way from others.—*St. Teresa.*

As the best honey is gathered from the flowers of the thyme, which is a small and bitter herb, so when virtues are exercised in the bitterness of the most humble tribulations, they become truly excellent.—*St. Francis de Sales.*

As the sun gives its heat no less to a rose amidst a thousand other flowers than if it were alone, so Our Lord does not diffuse His love the less upon one soul because He also loves an infinity of others. The power of His love never diminishes on account of the multitude of rays that it diffuses, but is always unchangeable in its immensity.—*The same.*

EXAMPLE

The Excellence of the 'Hail Mary'

The first Hail Mary pronounced by an Angel produced the greatest of all miracles, and was the source of the salvation of sinful men. If our redemption began with the Angelic Salutation, it follows that our salvation depends in a special manner upon this prayer. If it gave birth to the fruit of eternal life upon this dry and barren earth when it was brought by the messenger of Heaven, it will, if we recite it devoutly, give birth to Jesus Christ in our soul. It is a celestial dew which fertilizes souls, and those that are not refreshed by it do not produce fruit but only briars and thorns. The Most Holy Virgin made the following revelation to the Blessed Alan: 'Know, my son, and do not forget to make it known, that it is a probable sign of damnation to have tepidity, aversion, and negligence in the recital of the Angelical Salutation which brought salvation to the world.'

I know nothing, O Mary, says Thomas à Kempis, that is so glorious for you and so consoling for us as the Angelical Salutation: its sweetness is so great that no words can express it. Most certain it is, says another servant of Mary, that this prayer never ascends to Heaven without obtaining great favours for the body as well as the soul; because this tender Mother always responds with some grace when we salute her with the *Hail Mary*. The Blessed Virgin promised St. Gertrude as many favours at the hour of her death as she had recited *Ave Marias* during her life; and she also counselled St. Bridget to recite this prayer to obtain the pardon of some acts of impatience. We know that this Mother of Mercy taught St. Dominic the Holy Rosary as the most efficacious means for obtaining the conversion of heretics and sinners. And, in fact, the historians of that period relate that the first-fruits of this new devotion were manifested by the abjuration of more than a hundred thousand heretics, and the conversion of an incredible number of sinners.

Let us also quote the beautiful words of a Saint. 'The "*Ave Maria*," well recited, is the enemy that puts the devil to flight, and the weapon that kills him. It is the sanctification of the soul, the gladness of Angels, the melody of the predestinated, the Canticle of the New Testament, the joy of Mary, and the glory of the Most Holy Trinity. The *Ave Maria* is a celestial dew that fertilizes the soul, a beautiful rose which we present to Mary, and a precious pearl which we bestow upon her. Finally, it is the most magnificent eulogium which can be offered in her honour, and the attractions it possesses have so much power over her heart, that she is constrained to love him who recites it well.'

Another great servant of the Immaculate Virgin says of himself, that whenever he pronounced these words, *Hail Mary*, the world in his eyes lost all beauty, he felt an increase of Divine love, a more fervent devotion, more firmness in hope, greater joy, and a renewal of virtue and strength in his whole being.

Prayer of St. Bernard.—O sovereign Mistress of Angels and of men, to you do we turn our eyes! We must all appear one day before the Eternal Judge; alas! how shall we dare to present ourselves before Him, loaded as we are with so many sins, and who shall appease His just indignation? No one, O Mother of Mercy, can so assuredly do this but you who loved Him so much, and who were so tenderly loved by Him. Open then, O Mother of Grace, your compassionate ears to our sighs, and the bowels of your mercy to our tears; to you do we run as to our dear Mother. Ah! appease the just indignation of your Divine Son, and restore us to His favour. You do not abhor the sinner, nor do you reject him, however unworthy he may be, if, repentant, he implores your patronage. To you, then, do I have recourse, O my Mother; animate me to hope, sustain my weakness, abandon me not for a single instant, and reconcile me to my Eternal Judge, that I may be able to find mercy at the moment of my death. Amen.

Aspiration.—Monstra te esse matrem—Show me, O Mary, that you are my mother!

Practice.—Whatever contradiction you may meet with this day, accept it with resignation, and with the reflection that *God wills it.*

Nineteenth Day

Mary, at the Marriage of Cana, Teaches Us the Best Method of Prayer

'There was a marriage,' says St. John, 'in Cana of Galilee, and the Mother of Jesus was there. And Jesus also was invited and His disciples.'

Let us consider the goodness of our adorable Saviour in not refusing the invitation to the wedding. He had come to redeem and reform man, and therefore would not assume a rigid and austere manner. He was always gentle and courteous, so as to draw men to follow Him. His presence at the wedding was a restraint upon all levity and excesses that so often occur on these occasions. O faithful souls! what modesty must have reigned at these nuptials, in the presence of Our Lord and of the Most Holy Virgin! The failing of the wine was pre-ordained by the Will of God, Who wished, by a miracle, to manifest His power to those assembled, and in particular to His Apostles. The Most Holy Virgin, in her wisdom and prudence, knowing that the wine failed, was moved by the most ardent charity to find an expedient for supplying it. And how does she act? Well aware of the power and goodness of her Divine Son, and of His charity and mercy, she was certain that He would supply what was required, all the more as the married couple were not rich, and she knew He took pleasure in relieving the poor and conversing with them. She turned, therefore, to her Divine Son; and notice well how Our Blessed Lady acted, and what she said: *Vinum non habent*—'They have no wine.' These words imply, 'These good people are poor, and although their poverty is pleasing and dear to You, nevertheless, in itself, it is a misfortune, and is often the cause of confusion before men. You are Omnipotent, and can relieve their wants, and I doubt not Your charity and mercy will make some return for the kind invitation they have given us to assist at this feast by providing for them in their present need.' The Holy Virgin, however, did not utter so many words when she asked this miracle; she was most skilled in the art of praying well, and made use of the shortest and most suitable method that could be found, saying: 'They have no wine.' Mary speaks to Our Lord with the greatest possible reverence. She does not address Him in terms of arrogance or presumption, like many thoughtless and indiscreet persons when they ask, but she simply represents to Him the need of the guests, sure that He would hear her petition. What an excellent manner of prayer is this, to expose our necessities simply to God, and then abandon ourselves into His adorable hands, certain that He will succour us in that way which is most to our advantage! For instance, to say to Him: Lord, behold one of Thy poor creatures, who is desolate, afflicted, full of aridity, of miseries and sins, but Thou knowest my wants, and it is enough for me to manifest to Thee my state. To Thee it belongs to deliver me from so many miseries, in the manner and at the time that thou knowest to be most conducive to Thy glory and my salvation.

We may ask God, also, for temporal blessings; of this there is no doubt; for Our Lord Himself has taught us, in the *Our Father* to ask first that *the Kingdom of God may come* as the *end* to which we aspire, and that *His Holy Will be done* as the sole means to attain this *end*; and afterwards to ask Almighty God to *give us our daily bread* (*Panem nostrum quotidianum da nobis hodie*). Therefore Holy Church has authorized particular prayers for temporal blessings; for peace, in times of war; rain, in seasons of drought, and so on; and also special Masses for procuring relief in times of pestilence, and in other necessities. No doubt we can have recourse to God in all our wants, both spiritual and temporal, in two ways: by merely exposing to Him our necessities, as did the Most Holy Virgin, or by asking Him for that grace which in particular we require, but always with this condition, that *His Will be done and not ours*. And yet, in general, even when spiritual persons ask God for His holy love, which softens and lightens every difficulty, they take care not to include in their petition those virtues that mortify nature.

SPIRITUAL FLOWERS

However slight the services we render to the Blessed Virgin Mary, they are always dear to God, and He rewards them with eternal glory.—*St. Teresa.*

When you find yourself in any great difficulty, do not take any step without having first considered eternity.—*St. Francis de Sales.*

He who is capable of exercising mildness in sufferings, generosity under ill-treatment, and peace amidst discord, is almost perfect. Mildness, sweetness of heart, and evenness of temper are virtues as rare as is the virtue of chastity.—*The same.*

EXAMPLE

The Advantages of the 'Hail Mary'

After having considered in the preceding example the esteem in which this prayer was held by the Saints, let us now consider its advantages.

Mary rejoices greatly when she is addressed in the Angelical Salutation, as she herself revealed to St. Mechtild, saying that of all the honours that can be rendered her none is more pleasing, or gives more joy, than this prayer, to which are added the words, 'Holy Mary, Mother of God, pray for us sinners, etc.' This prayer reminds her of the obligation she is under to have compassion on poor sinners, to pray for them, to love them. Sinners are the occasion of all her happiness, 'because,' said she, 'I should not have found grace if they had not lost it; I should not have been chosen to be the Mother of the Saviour if it had not been necessary to save them; and lastly, I should not have received such an abundance of graces had it not been necessary that I should become the Mother of Mercy and the Refuge of Sinners.'

But the recitation of the *Hail Mary* does not form the joy of Mary alone; it is also the joy of the Angels and of the Saints. Blessed Alan says that the words of this prayer convey joy to all the inhabitants of heaven. The Angelical Salutation is the distinctive salute of the Angels to Mary; and these blessed spirits enjoy a special delight in offering it to her frequently every day. But whilst this admirable prayer causes all Paradise to exult with joy, and is a source of grace to faithful souls, it is also the terror of the demons, who take flight as soon as they hear it pronounced. When the *Hail Mary* was brought from heaven by an Angel, the earth leapt for joy, on account of its approaching deliverance. But hell seemed already to foresee the formidable presence of the Omnipotent Who was to destroy the empire of Satan; and it trembled with fear when this salutation was uttered. No wonder, then, that the impious, who are children of the accursed spirits, should adopt their sentiments and hate all that relates to the mystery of the Incarnation, and speak contemptuously of the Holy Rosary and of devotion to the Blessed Virgin. However, experience shows us that the more a soul gives signs of predestination, the more does she love, relish, and gladly recite the *Hail Mary*; and the more she loves God, the more does she love this prayer. 'I have no surer secret for ascertaining if a person love

God,' says the venerable Louis Marie de Montfort, 'than to examine if he love to recite the *Ave Maria* or the Rosary.'

Prayer.—Help us, O Mother full of mercy, and do not allow the multitude of our sins to weaken your love for us. Remember that our adorable Saviour deigned to take from you a mortal body, not to condemn but to save sinners. If it were for your own personal glory alone that you were chosen to be the Mother of God, it might be said that our eternal salvation, or damnation, matters but little to you; but it was for the salvation of all men that your Divine Son clothed Himself with our flesh. What advantage would accrue to us from your happiness and power if you did not make use of your power to render us partakers of your happiness? You know the need we have of your assistance; and therefore we recommend ourselves earnestly to you. Help us, that we may not have the misfortune to lose our souls, but may eternally love and serve your Divine Son with you in His kingdom of glory. Amen.

Aspiration.—Obtain for us, O Mary, by your powerful intercession, the grace not to lose the place which Our Saviour has prepared for us in Paradise.

Practice.—Ask Mary to obtain for you from God all the graces you are in need of today.

Twentieth Day

The Petition of Mary at the Marriage of Cana Was Full of Confidence

Let us endeavour, by the Divine assistance, to discover all the lessons contained in the petition of Mary and in the answer of Jesus.

Mary turns to Jesus, and says to Him: *Vinum non habent*—'They have no wine;' and He replies: *Quid mihi, et tibi est, mulier? Nondum venit hora mea*—'Woman, what is there in common between Me and thee? My hour is not yet come.'

This reply at first sight seems harsh, and it surprises us, coming from such a Son and addressed to such a Mother. Is it possible that so respectful a Son should reject with asperity a prayer made with so much reverence and humility by the most loving and the most loved of Mothers? Has the creature no part with her Creator from Whom she receives her being and her life? Has the Mother nothing to do with her Son, nor the Son with the Mother, from whom He received His Body and His Blood? These words seem, as I have said, somewhat strange, and are difficult to understand; indeed, they have been misinterpreted by some who, having kept merely to the letter, have unhappily originated several forms of heresy. However, the reply was most loving, and the Holy Virgin, who well understood its genuine sense, considered herself the happiest of Mothers. This she expressed, with a heart full of confidence, in her answer to the waiters. 'You have heard,' she said, 'the reply my Son has made me, and perhaps, not understanding the language of love, you fear that He is indignant at my petition; but it is not so, fear not; whatsoever He shall say to you, do ye'—*Quæcumque dixerit vobis, facite.*

The opinions of the Doctors upon the words of Our Blessed Saviour are various; many think that His meaning was: 'It does not belong to us to meddle in this affair; as we are merely amongst the invited, we should not observe what is required or not required at the wedding.' However, the greater number of the holy Fathers of the Church think that Our Lord thus replied to His Most Holy Mother, in order to teach those of high position in the Church not to make use of their influence in favour of their relations, in things which are contrary to the law of God or to the perfection of their state. To give this lesson to the world, He made use of the tender Heart of Mary, and, in doing so, He certainly gives us a very great proof of His love. His words signified that He knew well the tenderness and perfection of the love His Mother bore Him, and the firmness of her will, and therefore was well assured that the apparent harshness of His words would in no way trouble her soul. On this account the Most Holy Virgin did not lose confidence when she received His answer, but said to the waiters: 'Whatsoever He shall say to you, do ye.' Our Lord loves most tenderly those who abandon themselves, like His Most Holy Mother, completely to His care, allowing themselves to be governed by His Divine Providence, without caring whether the result be sweet or bitter, certain that the parental Heart of God will never permit the least thing to happen which will not turn to their advantage, if they have a perfect and filial confidence in Him. We ought, then, to imitate this example of Mary on all occasions, whether prosperous or adverse; allowing ourselves to be led by the Divine Will without ever seeking the accomplishment of our own. It is true that great confidence is necessary to enable us to abandon ourselves thus unreservedly to Divine Providence; but, if we do so, Our Lord takes care of everything, and conducts all for our advantage; while if we reserve something to ourselves, not confiding entirely in Him, then He abandons us. It is as if He were to say: You believe that you are capable of succeeding without My succour, therefore I shall withdraw, and you will see what will be the result.

This perfect abandonment must be grounded upon the infinite goodness of God, and upon the merits of the Passion and Death of Our Lord Jesus Christ, and accompanied by a firm and perfect resolution to give ourselves entirely to God leaving all things to His loving Providence.

SPIRITUAL FLOWERS

In Arabia Felix, not only the plants which are called aromatical are sweet scented, but all plants without distinction, because they all experience the influence of the sun's intense heat. So all the works of a soul that is replenished with charity or the virtue of holy love, even the very least, have a most pleasing fragrance before the Divine Majesty, Who rewards them with an increase of charity.—*St. Francis de Sales.*

If you sincerely love God, you will often speak of Him. As bees gather honey only with their mouths, so your tongue will be always honeyed with the words you speak of your God; and never will your mouth taste such sweetness as when you sing the praises and blessings of His Most Holy Name.—*The same.*

As some herbs, when well masticated, produce so great sweetness as to appease hunger and thirst, so one who receives from God the celestial manna of interior consolation cannot in any way desire the consolations of the world, though it be only to receive a momentary satisfaction.—*The same.*

EXAMPLE

Further Advantages of the 'Hail Mary'

Let us glory, says a pious author, in repeating this salutation with the Angel Gabriel, the Apostles, the Martyrs, and all the Christian world. Let this *Ave Maria*, which comes to us fragrant as a Canticle of heaven, and repeated by as many echoes as there are faithful souls on earth, be sweet to our lips, and sweeter still to our hearts. It is a rare and enviable favour indeed to be able to salute a queen, and yet every day, at every moment, men and women, old and young, all of every condition, can salute the Queen of heaven and earth, who contains in her hands all the treasures of God, and can be sure of being always heard, and that each salutation addressed to her will meet with a corresponding benefit. . . . But can the sinner also dare to approach her? Yes, certainly; let him also come with humble confidence and salute her who is his refuge, for she will in no wise be offended by his prayer; and if the *Hail Mary* from his lips be a cry of sorrow and repentance, it will become omnipotent, and will obtain mercy, pardon, grace, and salvation.

Hail Mary! *Ave Maria!* . . . A sweet and beautiful word it is, which heaven sent to earth, and earth again returns so frequently to heaven!

The *Ave Maria* is the universal prayer of each and all. The infant begins to lisp it, and on his knees, with his hands raised to heaven, says *Ave Maria!* The aged, weakened by infirmity, may be incapable of reciting long prayers, but they will always have sufficient strength to repeat devoutly the *Ave Maria*. This is the favourite prayer of just souls. Oh, how many times in the day does it rise from their hearts full of burning love, and ascend, like purest burning incense to the throne of Mary! *Ave Maria!* . . . it is also the prayer of sinners, and perhaps their only prayer. In the great number of these there are some, alas! who have forgotten all other prayers, but they still know and repeat the *Ave Maria*. Yes; amidst the universal wreck of all other prayers and practices of religion, the *Ave Maria* or *Hail Mary* has remained for them ever a means of salvation. . . . How many poor wrecked souls have been led back to the haven of salvation by this means!

Prayer.—O Jesus! only Son of God, Who from the bosom of Thy Eternal Father, descended into the bosom of Mary, Thy Mother, receive the homage of my adoration and love. Through Thee I go to Thy Father, and through Thy Mother I come to Thee. Like the spouses at Cana, I dare not address my prayer directly to Thee, but I fear nothing when I direct it through Thy Blessed Mother. O Lord! well Thou knowest that I have no wine, no courage, nor strength, nor holy and generous resolutions; I have lost all! Ah! say not to Thy Mother, who intercedes in my favour: 'Woman, what is there in common between us?' because I know for certain that she is all-powerful over Thy filial Heart. Add not 'My hour is not yet come!' Ah, no; Thy hour, O my God, to benefit those who pray to Thee, through Thy Blessed Mother, is ever at hand. O Lord! behold, the vessel of my heart is full of the insipid waters of earth; change this water into the delicious wine of holy affections for heaven, where the Saints celebrate the nuptials of the Lamb amidst eternal joys. Amen.

Aspiration.—Succour my weakness, O most powerful Virgin!

Practice.—Endeavour to preserve confidence in God, when He delays the graces you desire.

Twenty-First Day

Mary Obtains the First Miracle from Jesus by Her Lively Faith

That we may conceive a just idea of the power the Most Holy Virgin possesses over the Heart of Jesus, let us meditate upon those other words which He addressed to her at the marriage of Cana: *Nondum venit hora mea*—'My hour is not yet come.'

Without discussing the opinion of certain Doctors, who think that Our Lord, by these words, meant to say that the wine was not yet wanted, I shall call your attention to this reflection: that there are certain times ordained by Divine Providence upon which our conversion and salvation depend.

It is certain that God had from all eternity determined the hour and moment when He would work the great miracle of His Incarnation, and give to the world the first sign of His power, but yet this determination could be accelerated by prayer.

The greater number of the Fathers assert that Mary, by her loving sighs and aspirations, merited the acceleration of the Incarnation of Our Lord. Not, indeed, that

He became Incarnate before the time that He had determined, but that, from all eternity He foresaw that the Holy Virgin would beg Him to hasten the time of His coming into the world; and therefore, in consideration of the great merit of her intercession, He ordained to become Man sooner than He would have done had He not been petitioned to do so. The same may be said of the first miracle, wrought by Our Lord at the wedding of Cana. *Nondum venit hora mea*—'My hour is not yet come,' said Jesus to His Holy Mother, but as I can refuse you nothing, I shall hasten to hear your prayer.

Oh, how precious is that hour in which Divine Providence wills to impart to us those special graces and blessings that are necessary for our salvation, Happy the soul who awaits this hour patiently, and who endeavours to prepare herself for it when it arrives. The Samarian woman assuredly was converted at this hour, and upon its arrival will depend also our own conversion and spiritual regeneration. We will now consider how Our Lord acted when He worked this miracle.

In the hall were seven stone urns, prepared for the purification, practised by the Jews. Our Lord ordered them to be filled with water, *Implete hydrias aqua*; and as the waiters had already been directed by Mary to follow punctually the orders of her Divine Son, they filled them 'up to the brim,' as the Sacred Text expresses it. Afterwards Our Saviour said something interiorly, not understood by anyone, and the water was instantly changed into most excellent wine. These words which He spoke were similar, without doubt, to those by which He drew all things out of nothing, or by which He gave being and life to man, or by which, also, at His last supper with His disciples, He changed wine into His adorable Blood, and thus instituted the Most Holy Sacrament of the Eucharist, giving to us, through it, that most excellent wine which nourishes us for eternal life.

This fact in the Gospel shows us, moreover, the great confidence we should have in the powerful intercession of Our Lady. But in order that she may represent our necessities to her Divine Son, we must invite her and our adorable Saviour to our banquet, because wine can never fail when Jesus and Mary are present; this Mother of Mercy being ever prepared to ask it for us, and her Divine Son ever ready to bestow it.

However, if we desire Our Lady to intercede with her Divine Son that He may change the water of our tepidity into the wine of His fervent love, we must imitate the waiters at the marriage of Cana, and do all that Our Lord shall tell us. Obey Him, then, with fidelity, O ye servants of God, fill your hearts well with the penitential water of repentance, and He will change it into the wine of His holy love. In order to obtain the spirit of fervour, nourish your mind with holy thoughts; make frequent aspirations, and, as a general rule, if you wish to be recollected in time of prayer, avoid dissipation during the day, and waste no time in useless reflections upon yourself, or on what happens around you. Keep yourself in the presence of God, and repose in the loving arms of His Providence. Bless this adorable Providence continually during life, and you will glorify It eternally in heaven, with all the Saints and blessed spirits.

SPIRITUAL FLOWERS

The Spouse in the Canticles says that her hands distil myrrh—a liquor which preserves from corruption; her eyes are like those of the dove, in their purity; from her ears hang pendants of gold, as a sign of chastity; her lips are vermilion, the symbol of her modesty in speech; and her nose like the tower of Lebanon, of incorruptible wood. Such should be the devout servant of God—chaste, pure and unspotted in her whole soul and body.—*St. Francis de Sales.*

Clasp Jesus closely to your breast; let Him be a beautiful and sweet bouquet of flowers upon your heart, so that whoever approaches you may be conscious of the perfume, and know that the fragrance of your life should be of myrrh—the symbol of mortification.—*The same.*

Keep always close to Jesus Crucified, in spirit, in meditation, and in reality by Holy Communion. As he who is accustomed to lie down upon a certain species of herb becomes chaste and pure, so your soul and your heart will be very quickly purified from every spot and from every unruly desire when Our Lord, Who is the true Lamb of God, reposes upon your heart.—*The same.*

EXAMPLE

Most Pleasing to Our Blessed Lord Is Our Devotion to His Mother

St. Teresa relates the following:

> 'Don Bernadino de Mendoza, to testify his devotion to the Most Holy Virgin, came to offer me his house, at Pico de Olmos, near Valladolid, for a Convent of Our Lady of Carmel. To say the truth, I felt some repugnance to found a religious house far from a town, yet the offering had been made so cordially, and for so holy a purpose, that

I considered I ought not to refuse it, and thus deprive the young gentleman of so much merit.

'About two months afterwards he was seized by a mortal illness, deprived of the power of speech, and died without having been able to make his confession. The Divine Master then said to me: "His salvation, my dear daughter, was in great danger; but I showed him mercy, in reward of the house he had made over for the foundation of a Convent consecrated to My Mother, under the title of Carmel. However, he will not be released from Purgatory until the first Mass is celebrated in that Convent."

'From that time my mind was ever occupied with the thought of his sufferings. The foundation of Valladolid could not be formed as quickly as I desired. One day, when I was stopping at St. Joseph's, at Medina del Campo, whilst I was at prayer, Our Lord said to me: "Make haste, because this soul suffers much." After this nothing could induce me to delay. Being arrived at Valladolid, although the house was unhealthy, I prepared some cells, just for the time being, and provided merely what was absolutely necessary. When Sunday arrived, notwithstanding the delay of the formal authorization, permission was granted to have Mass celebrated on the spot which was destined for the Church. I did not, indeed, believe that the promise of Our Lord regarding this gentleman would be fulfilled then; on the contrary, I was persuaded that the words, *until the first Mass*, related to that Mass when the Blessed Sacrament would be reserved for the first time in the Church. But when the Priest turned towards us, with the sacred ciborium in his hand, to communicate us, and I had approached the Altar to receive the sacred Host, I saw the gentleman by the side of the Priest, full of joy and resplendent with light. He thanked me for all I had done to deliver him from the flames of Purgatory, and then ascended to heaven.

'Oh, how precious is any service, however small, that we are able to render the Most Holy Virgin! Who can tell how pleasing it is to Our Lord, and how mercifully He rewards it?'

Prayer.—O Mother! full of love and clemency towards us, you are penetrated with the same sentiments as your Divine Son, and you also say with Him: 'Whenever the sinner returns to me with sincere sorrow for his offences, he always finds me ready to receive him with kindness and tenderness. I think not of the malice, or the number of his sins, but I only look at the desire he has to be converted; and I am always disposed to implore a remedy for his wounds, because I am, in deed and in name, the Mother of Grace and of Mercy!'

O Mary! since you never reject the sinner who returns to you with a resolution to amend, and since you have the power, as well as the will, to obtain the cure of all the wounds of the heart, behold me at your feet, full of confidence. Behold, I beseech you, the deep and cankered wounds of my soul, and if you will deign to offer your prayers to your Divine Son for me, I shall hope everything for my eternal salvation. Amen.

Aspiration.—Through your intercession, O tender Mother, I hope to obtain the eternal happiness of heaven!

Practice.—Let all the good works of this day be directed to obtain the conversion of sinners.

Twenty-Second Day

Mary Chose the Better Part

We read in the Gospel that Martha, into whose house Our Lord had entered, was busy and troubled about many things in her anxiety to serve Him, whilst her sister Mary remained at His feet, listening to His words. Martha was concerned about Our Lord's bodily comfort, but Mary, laying aside every other thought, nourished her soul with the sacred instructions of her Divine Master. A soul, recollected interiorly before God, is sometimes so sweetly attentive to the goodness of her Beloved as not even to be aware of its attentiveness, so simply and gently is it exercised. Such souls are like those who navigate rivers the waters of which flow on so calmly that they neither see nor feel any motion. This delightful repose of the soul is called by St. Teresa 'The Prayer of Quiet.'

Martha, moved by a slight sentiment of envy (which is an almost universal vice, affecting even devout souls), complained thus to Our Lord: 'Master, hast Thou no care that my sister hath left me alone to serve? Speak to her, therefore, that she help me.' Our Lord, Who is Infinite Goodness, would not reprehend her seriously, although He knew the imperfection of her sentiments, but He called her by name, gently and affectionately (for the whole Gospel is love), and said to her: 'Martha, Martha, thou art careful and troubled about many things; but one thing is necessary. Mary has chosen the better part, which shall not be taken from her!'—*Martha, Martha, sollicita es et turbaris erga plurima; porro unum est necessarium. Maria optimam partem elegit, quæ non auferetur ab ea.*

Whilst Martha was thus busy serving Our Divine Saviour, Mary had but one thought—to remain with Him and hear His words. This was also the one thought of Our Blessed Lady, the Most Holy Virgin. Observe her at Bethlehem, where all her efforts to find a lodging were vain; she says not a word, utters no complaint, but retires into a stable and places the newborn Infant in a manger! After a few days the Magi come to adore Him, and she receives in silence the praises addressed to her. She flies into Egypt, but shows no sign of grief; she returns to Judea without any manifestation of joy. On Calvary, at the feet of her Divine Son, she opens not her mouth, but listens to His words, for to hear them is all her desire. Indifferent to all things else, 'happen what will,' says she, 'whether He console me or afflict me, I am equally contented, provided I be near Him and possess Him.'

Thus does a soul abandoned to the Will of God remain in His arms, like a child on the bosom of his mother. When she places him on the ground he walks, and when she takes him again in her arms he allows himself to be carried, and is in no way troubled to know whither he is taken. Thus the soul cultivates tranquillity of heart, and advances continually in union with the Divine Goodness.

The exercise of union with God can be practised by means of short but frequent aspirations of the soul to God, such as: 'Ah, Jesus, who will give me to be but one spirit with Thee? I renounce all creatures and desire Thee alone, for this is the one thing needful. Ah! plunge my soul into the ocean of Thy Goodness, from whence it proceeds, and make me, O Lord, wholly Thine. Draw me, and I will run after Thy attractions, casting myself into Thy paternal arms, and never again withdrawing myself from them.'

A soul immersed in God dies not. How could it die if immersed in Him Who is life? It lives, then, but not in itself. As the planets do not shine in the presence of the sun, but the sun shines in them, so does it live, not, indeed, a natural life, but the life of Jesus Christ, Who lives in it.

In imitation of the Blessed Virgin we must make it our whole study to unite ourselves to Our Lord by advancing in perfection. Let us not, however, forget that our best means for attaining to this is to remain tranquil, and place all our confidence in Him Who alone can give increase to that which we have sown and planted. Our Lord desires from us a peaceful solicitude, which will lead us to obey those who direct us and walk with all fidelity in the paths they point out. We should abandon ourselves in all things to His Paternal care, and maintain peace of soul as far as possible, because Our Lord reposes in tranquil and peaceful hearts. When the waters of a lake are not agitated by the wind, the firmament with its stars is so vividly represented therein that, looking down into the deep, we can see its beauty as perfectly as if we were looking up to the heavens. So also when our souls are tranquil and undisturbed by superfluous cares or distractions, we are then well prepared to receive within us the image of Our Lord. But if the soul be disquieted, darkened, and agitated by the various tempests of the passions, and allows itself to be guided by them, and not by reason, which renders us like to God, it cannot reflect the beautiful image of

Jesus Christ Crucified and His most excellent virtues, nor can He rest in the soul. We must abandon the thought of ourselves to Divine Providence, for anxiety of mind and the desire to know if we advance in virtue is not pleasing to God, and serves only to satisfy self-love, which is a great busybody that seeks to have a hand in everything. One work well done with peace of mind is more meritorious than many works performed with agitation and anxiety.

SPIRITUAL FLOWERS

When the lily springs up from the earth it produces a number of long leaves, but as it grows higher the leaves near the flower are fewer and much smaller. These leaves represent our words. The more a soul progresses in the way of God and of perfection the fewer are her words.—*Père St. Jure.*

As the bees go all round their hive gathering honey here and there, and when they have collected it take pleasure in working it up, on account of its sweetness, so we meditate that we may acquire the love of God; and then we contemplate Him, and are attracted by His goodness through the sweetness which His love causes us to experience. Hence the soul is never satiated with considering and looking upon the Divine Beauty.—*St. Francis de Sales.*

The occupations that are necessary for each one in his state of life are no hindrance to piety, but increase it and adorn the work of devotion. The nightingale loves its own melody when it is silent as much as when it sings; the devout heart also cherishes Divine love no less when it is distracted by the external duties of life than when it prays. Its action and its contemplation, its occupation, as well as its repose, equally chant the canticle of love.—*The same.*

EXAMPLE

Beauty of the 'Ave Maris Stella'

In this hymn are celebrated all the prerogatives of Mary. She is the powerful Mother of God and the most glorious of Virgins—*Dei Mater alma atque semper Virgo*—and at the same time the most sweet and humble of Virgins—*Virgo singularis inter omnes mitis.*

The Most Holy Virgin performs the function of advocate with her Divine Son in our favour, and offers Him our prayers—*Monstra te esse Matrem.*

She is the Gate of Heaven. She loosens the chains of sinners, guides the blind in the way of virtue, removes every kind of evil from us, and asks in our name for every grace necessary for us to reach the port of eternal life.—*Solve vincla reis.*

Nothing is more appropriate to inspire us with a tender confidence in Mary than the *Ave Maris Stella*, for its verses contain considerations of time and eternity. Let us, then, repeat it often, and Mary will load us with benedictions, as many miraculous facts in the lives of the Saints attest. Indeed, this Queen of Heaven herself showed how dear to her is this hymn when she appeared one day to St. Bridget, and thus addressed her: 'My Son, the Sovereign Master of heaven, of earth, and of hell, can Himself alone suppress all the powers of evil, from whatever source they may arise. I shall henceforth be a shield of defence for you and for the others against all the attempts of the enemies of your souls and bodies, on condition, however, that all your community meet together to sing every evening the *Ave Maris Stella.*'

The Saint did not fail to fulfil punctually the will of the Most Holy Virgin, and her example was followed by her Confessor, and her daughter, St. Catherine of Sweden, who caused this pious practice to be adopted by all the convents of the Order of St. Saviour. Let us then be glad to salute our most amiable Mother frequently with this hymn of the holy Abbot of Clairvaux. However, we must not be satisfied with merely singing it; let us also carry it in our minds and in our hearts; and, above all, strive to be penetrated with all the affectionate sentiments it contains. Let us pray to St. Bernard to recommend us himself to the Queen of Angels, and obtain for us that she may be to us all that she was to him to the last instant of his life. Most Blessed Virgin! be my strength, my guide, my Mother! and let me never become unworthy to bear the beautiful title of Child of Mary. *Monstra te esse Matrem.*

Prayer.—O Holy Virgin and Mother of God! deign to succour those who implore your assistance. Cast an eye of compassion upon us, and be moved at the sight of our miseries. O Mother of Grace! have you forgotten men in their tribulations and need, by reason of the sublime dignity to which you have been raised? No, without doubt your heart will be ever interested in our favour, nor can your great mercy ever forget misery so profound as ours. Turn then towards us, and consider the many dangers to which we are continually exposed. God Almighty has constituted you the depositary of

His power and of His graces; pour them upon us in abundance, we beg of you. The more powerful you are, the more do I trust, O Mother of Mercy, that you will be singularly merciful to your afflicted children who have recourse to you. Amen.

Aspiration.—O Mary! you are able to succour me, and I hope your goodness will not refuse me this favour.

Practice.—Endeavour to recollect yourself frequently during the day, that you may act with greater purity of intention.

Twenty-Third Day

The Blessed Virgin Did Not Neglect the Duties of Martha

The conduct of Martha and Mary give us another touching subject for our meditation. These two sisters well represent to us Our Lady. Like Martha the Blessed Virgin Mary received her Son Our Lord into her house, and into her most chaste womb, when He came into this world, and with incomparable care she always served Him whilst He lived on earth, in reward of which He exalted her in heaven to an unparalleled glory. Like Mary, she listened to His words in uninterrupted silence, and occupied herself only in loving Him. This glorious Virgin exercised admirably in the course of her life the offices of both of these sisters. But as regards the office of Martha, with what care and attention did she not serve Our Lord when an Infant! What diligence did she employ in avoiding the anger of Herod, and all the dangers with which His life was threatened!

Take notice that Our Lord reprehended Martha because she was disturbed and troubled, not because she was careful. Our Lady, like Martha, took great care to serve our Divine Master well—but her care was devoid of all disquiet and anxious trouble. The Saints in heaven are zealous for the glory of God, but are not disquieted. The Angels are careful in all that regards our salvation, and God Himself has care of His creatures, but always in peace and undisturbed calm. To us, miserable creatures, however, this is difficult. Some become suddenly disturbed because they cannot do what they desire; others wish to console and visit the sick, but if they meet with some hindrance they are immediately troubled; others will have a great affection for mental prayer, and although this relates only to God, yet even here human nature enters, and they will be disturbed and troubled if they are constrained to occupy themselves in some other employment.

Now would Martha have been so much troubled if she had had no other end in view than to please Our Lord? No, certainly; because one only kind of food, well prepared, was sufficient for His nourishment, and, moreover, because she saw that the whole pleasure of her Divine Master was to be listened to, as was done by her sister Mary. But Martha mingled a little self-esteem with her desire to provide all that was necessary for our Divine Master; and this moved her to wish that her hospitality, in receiving those who honoured her with their visits, should be recognised. The good lady believed that by this external service she would become a great servant of God, and surpass others; and through love for her sister she wished that she also should be solicitous to serve the Beloved Master, and thus, as she thought, acquire more merit. But our Divine Redeemer was more pleased with the practice of Mary, into whose heart He poured forth, through His divine words, graces surpassing all conception. This was the truth He wished also to inculcate, when He said, that those alone were blessed who should have listened to His word and practised it.

All that anxious restlessness and eager desire to do something for Our Lord, which some devout persons look upon as real virtue, is then a manifest error, reproved by our Divine Master, when He said: *Porro unum est necessarium*—'But one thing is necessary.'

You may ask, in reply, But how are we to prevent being uneasy when we are under an obligation of practising virtue? This solicitude is certainly not blamable, provided it be not overanxious and troubled. Invoke frequently the one beautiful Dove of the Heavenly Spouse, that she may truly obtain for you the heart of a dove, and that you may not only be a dove in your flight towards heaven, by prayer, but also a dove in your nest, and with all those who surround you. Unite the office of Mary with that of Martha: diligently fulfil the duties of your state. Often cast yourself at the feet of Jesus, and say to Him from your heart: O my Divine Master, whether I go or stay, I am all Thine and Thou art all mine. Thou art my only Spouse, and all that I am going to do shall be for Thee.

As the birds have their nests in which to hide themselves when needful, so our heart should select and take possession of some spot every day, either on Calvary or in the Sacred Wounds of Our Lord, or near Him, whither it may retire on every occasion to defend itself in temptations and recreate itself after the many exterior affairs of the day. Happy the soul that can truly say to Our Lord: You are my house of refuge, my secure home; my roof, in time of rain, and my refreshment under burning heats.

A remedy, however, against so many anxious cares and troubles is to copy the practice of Mary, because it was praised by Our Lord Himself, Who called it the best and the one thing necessary. Now, this one thing necessary is nothing else than the exercise of Divine Love, which, as it contains in itself the perfection of all other virtues, produces their acts in due time and place, according to circumstances. In one word, then: *Possess holy Charity, and no virtue will be wanting to you, because all virtues are comprised in Charity.*

SPIRITUAL FLOWERS

The Most Holy Virgin Mary is compared to an orange-tree laden with fruit, and diffusing the sweetest odour of Lebanon. This means that all her thoughts, words, and actions were so perfect that, like an exquisite perfume, they delighted both Heaven and earth: and that, like the pomegranate, they wore the crown of perfection.—*Père S. Jure.*

The bee sucks honey from flowers without injuring them, and leaves them as entire and fresh as he found them. Devotion has this higher excellence, that it adds new beauty to all that it touches.—*St. Francis de Sales.*

Remember that when the bees make honey, they take bitter food; so, also, we can never make acts of greater patience and sweetness, nor form better the honey of excellent virtues than by eating the bread of bitterness and living a life of tribulation.—*The same.*

EXAMPLE

The 'Magnificat'

The *Magnificat* is the first Canticle of the New Testament and the most magnificent Canticle of Holy Scripture. It presents us with most sublime ideas of the greatness of God, and is sung on solemn festivals, whilst Priests stand and incense the Altar.

We recite the *Magnificat* to thank God for all the graces bestowed upon the Most Holy Virgin. It is the only work she ever composed, and contains mysteries far surpassing our understanding. Hence this proverb was familiar amongst the ancient authors when they spoke of one who meddled with things beyond his capacity; such a one would *correct the Magnificat.*

The Blessed Juliana had a special affection for this Canticle. Speaking of it one day to the Superior of a convent, she declared that she would not sacrifice the sweetness she experienced in reciting it for all the gold that the convent could contain. She repeated it nine times a day, in memory of the nine months that the Most Holy Virgin bore the Redeemer of the world in her womb; and she desired ardently that all would follow her example, believing it impossible that Mary would not hear those who share in the joy she manifests in this Canticle.

Cardinal J. de Vitry, in the life of Ste. Marie de Ogniez, relates that when this Saint was near death, and was singing the *Magnificat*, the Mother of God appeared to her and told her to receive Extreme Unction, and she remained by her bedside in company with her Divine Son until the Saint expired.

St. Anselm relates of himself that when he was afflicted with various infirmities, which occasioned him the most acute suffering, he was perfectly cured by reciting the *Magnificat.*

Prayer.—August Mother of God, you are the Queen of Mercy, and I am the most miserable of sinners, and consequently your subject. You should then have greater compassion for me than for anyone less sinful. *Eia ergo advocata nostra, illos tuos misericordes oculos ad nos converte.*

O, our refuge and our advocate, turn one look of mercy towards us; interest yourself in our behalf; be moved to compassion for our evils, and obtain their cure. Deliver us from our miseries, and we shall never cease to sing the hymn of praise to your mercy, of which we have experienced the salutary effects. Amen.

Aspiration.—Pray for me, O Mother of Grace, O Mother of Mercy!

Practice.—Whilst you fulfil the duties of your state in imitation of Martha, endeavour to have your mind and heart turned to Jesus as Mary had.

Twenty-Fourth Day

Mary in Her Sleep

We can begin to love God in this life, but it is only in the next that we shall be able to love Him perfectly. In the expression *we* I do not intend to speak of the Most Holy Virgin, because she is the Daughter of beautiful Love, the one only dove, the perfect Spouse. Yes; the charity of Mary surpassed that of the Seraphim. 'If all the daughters have gathered riches, thou hast surpassed them all.'

The Saints and Angels are compared to stars, but Mary is beautiful as the moon, distinguished amidst the Saints as the moon amidst the stars. As her charity surpasses in heaven that of all the blessed, so did she exercise it with greater excellence on earth; for never having sinned, even venially, her love never met with any obstacle, and thus increased at every instant. What progress, then, must she not have made in the exercise of holy love? Say not that the Most Holy Virgin, like all men, was subject to the necessities of life. It may be said, in the words of the Canticles, that her sleep was the sleep of Love, the celestial Spouse saying, *'I adjure you, daughters of Jerusalem, that you stir not nor awake my love till she please.'*

The Queen of heaven and earth granted to her chaste body that repose only which was necessary to restore its strength, in order to serve God more perfectly; and we may say that her sleep never interrupted the exercise of holy love, because it proceeded from an act of most excellent charity. Does not St. Augustine teach that we must love our body, that it may serve us in those works which God requires of us, and because it forms part of ourselves, and is one day to share our eternal felicity?

The Most Holy Virgin, indeed, had other reasons to love her body with a virtuous love, because it was not only pure, submissive, and docile to all the functions of holy love and embalmed by Divine sweetness, but it was, moreover, the living source of the Sacred Body of Our Saviour. Thus it belonged to her in an incomparably singular manner, so that before yielding to sleep she could truly say to it, 'Rest from your fatigues, O throne of the Divinity, tabernacle of the new Covenant, ark of all Sanctity; recruit your strength through the repose which I allow you to take.'

Ah! sweet Jesus! what must have been the thoughts of your Most Holy Mother whilst sleep refreshed her body and her heart was watching! We may imagine that her most frequent thought was of her Divine Son, Who had so often slept upon her bosom as the lamb reposes upon the soft wool of its mother. She would also feel that she rested in His adorable side, opened by the lance on Calvary, as a white dove rests in the cleft of a rock. Thus her sleep, which was a sweet repose and an agreeable solace to her body, became a kind of ecstasy to her soul, through the spiritual effects and operations it produced.

If she also represented to herself her future glory, like Joseph, the saviour of Egypt, and saw herself clothed with the sun and the moon under her feet—that is to say, surrounded by the glory of her Divine Son, and resplendent with the glory of the Saints who form her crown as she rules over the universe, of which she is the Queen; or if, like Jacob, she foresaw the wonderful fruits that Angels and men would obtain through the Redemption, O! conceive, if possible, children of Mary, the delights caused by such spiritual entertainments!

There is one kind of diamond which has this special property—that nothing can diminish its fine water or the brilliancy which nature has given it. The Heart of the Virgin Mother, like this diamond, never ceased to glow with the sacred fire of love that she had received from her Divine Son. However, though the brilliancy of precious stones does not diminish, yet it does not increase; whilst the love of the Most Holy Virgin never remained in the same state, but made continual and incredible progress until she entered heaven. With good reason, then, is Our Lady called the Mother of pure Love—that is to say, the most lovable amongst all creatures, and the most beloved by her only Son, Who is loved by her as the most lovable and loving of Sons.

SPIRITUAL FLOWERS

Forgetfulness of God is the sleep of the soul. The soul has been asleep all the time that it has forgotten its God.—*St. Augustine.*

The sleep of the Saints is a prayer before God.—*St. Jerome.*

It is great blindness and misery to seek repose where it is impossible to find it.—*St. Teresa.*

EXAMPLE

Devotion to the 'Salve Regina'

St. Bernard is celebrated for his love of the Blessed Virgin and for the praises he has rendered to her. His language is of such sweetness, that it surpasses that of all preceding ages for beauty and tenderness in discoursing of the Blessed Virgin Mary. This saint seems to have gathered together and made his own all the most loving affections of the most fervent servants. Mary was his ruling thought, and he could not restrain the transports of his heart when he spoke of her. The very mention of her name sufficed to render him ecstatic. With good reason, then, did Peter the Abbot of St. Remigius, at Rheims, say to one of St. Bernard's adversaries: 'If you have the courage to touch the pupil of Mary's eye, write against St. Bernard.'

This Saint was commissioned to preach the second general Crusade throughout Europe, and when he had traversed France, Belgium and the Rhenish countries, he retired to the Abbey of Effinghem, to recollect his soul in that pious solitude. One evening the Monks were moved to tears by a discourse of St. Bernard's in praise of Mary, and they begged him to intone the *Salve Regina*, which they sang every evening before her image. As the Saint could not excuse himself, he devoutly intoned the *Salve* with his powerful voice, and was accompanied by all the Monks. When the sweet words *Et Jesum benedictum fructum ventris tui, nobis post hoc exilium ostende* had been sung, all were silent (because at that time the anthem ended with these words). However, the inspired voice of Bernard continued, and he gave expression to the sentiments of his heart in the three invocations with which it is now concluded: *O clemens, O pia, O dulcis Virgo Maria!* These words were afterwards adopted by the whole Church.

It is in commemoration of this event that the *Salve Regina* is solemnly sung every evening in the Cathedral of Spire.

St. Vincent de Paul used to say that no prayer is so suitable to us miserable exiles in this valley of tears as this: *Salve Regina, Mater misericordiæ . . . Ad te clamamus, exules filii Hevæ.*

St. Philip Neri, having heard the confession of a famous criminal, spoke thus to him: 'My son, I shall require but little from you, and if you fulfil it I assure you that you will be saved. Promise me to place all your confidence in the Most Blessed Virgin, the Mother of Divine Grace, and for this purpose recite the *Salve*

Regina seven times every day in her honour, and kiss the ground the same number of times, saying: "I may die this moment."' The penitent made the promise and kept it. He died holily fourteen years after, full of gratitude and love towards his good Mother Mary.

Prayer.—Most amiable Heart of Mary, object of the complacency of the adorable Trinity, and worthy of the veneration of Angels and of men; Heart like unto that of Jesus Christ and its most perfect image; Heart full of goodness and compassion for our miseries! Oh, break the ice of our hearts, turn our affections towards the adorable Heart of Our Saviour, and impress on them the love of your virtues. Watch over Holy Church, protect it, and be to it an impregnable fortress, so that it may be secure amidst all the assaults of its enemies. Be you our way to God, our succour in our trials, our consolation in sufferings, our strength in temptations, and our refuge in persecutions. Above all things assist us at the point of death, when hell will exert all its efforts for our eternal ruin. Let us then, indeed, experience the power you have over the Heart of Jesus, that we may find a secure asylum in the bosom of His Mercy, and then, with you, praise Him throughout ages and ages. Amen.

Aspiration.—I sleep, O Mother, but my heart watches.

Practice.—Endeavour to be reflecting upon some eternal truth when you fall asleep.

Twenty-Fifth Day

Mary on Calvary Is the Mother of All Christians

Our Beloved Saviour had instituted the Sacrament of Love that He might remain amid His children. He had poured forth all His Blood for us, and He wished moreover to bequeath us a legacy in the last Testament of His Love. But what more could He give us? He casts a compassionate look upon His tender Mother, who stands immovable at the foot of the Cross with His beloved disciple. It is not to enrich her with His grace, for she already possessed it most excellently; nor is it to promise her glory, she was sure of it; but it is to infuse into her heart, before He died, a more tender and ardent love for men than she yet possessed. 'Woman,' says He to her, pointing to the beloved disciple, *'behold your son!'* What an exchange was this! The servant instead of the Only Son—the creature in place of the Creator! And yet she does not refuse it, well knowing that she accepted for her children, in the person of John, all the followers of the Cross of Jesus, and that she was to become the beloved Mother of all Christians.

Although Our Lady gave birth to none but our adorable Saviour, yet, in a spiritual sense, she brought forth all Christians in the Person of Our Saviour; because this Blessed Seed has begotten us all by His death. A seed when planted produces a tree, from which are produced other seeds, all of which may be said to belong to the original fruit from which the tree came forth. Thus, as the Most Holy Virgin brought forth this mystic Seed, which when cast on earth, budded and brought forth many other seeds, she has consequently brought us all forth and has become the Mother of us all. How much we ought to love the Son and the Mother! for they are our Divine parents, and it is impossible to love one without loving the other.[4]

As Holy Church wishes to teach us to go to Jesus through Mary, she directs that the Angelical Salutation should follow the *Our Father*, that we may thus

---

4 Happy the soul who, like a good child in regard of her parents, sees only Jesus and Mary, converses only with Jesus and Mary, and whose only joy and desire in this world is to know Mary in Jesus and Jesus in Mary. This is a wonderful means, given us by God, of spending our lives holily during our sorrowful sojourn in this present life.—(J. J. OLIER.)

petition, through her, for all benefits, both spiritual and temporal, as far as these latter are conducive to our eternal salvation. We also implore the intercession of Mary in order to receive the Holy Ghost, as it was through her that St. Elizabeth received His gifts.

Honour and revere with especial love the holy and glorious Virgin Mary, for she is the Mother of Our God and Saviour Jesus Christ, and therefore our most excellent Mother. Let us then have recourse to her as little children; let us cast ourselves upon her bosom on every occasion, and at every moment, with perfect confidence. Let us appeal to her maternal love, endeavour to imitate her virtues, and cherish in our heart the true sentiments of children.

In the ancient Law much honour was paid to the Ark, in which were preserved the manna, the rod of Aaron, and the tables of the Law. With much greater reason should we honour this living Ark of the new Covenant. Indeed, what does the manna prefigure but the Divinity of the Son of God, come down from heaven to unite Himself with our humanity? He is, also, the Miraculous Rod and the Living Stone upon which the commandments of the Law of Grace were written, being engraved upon His Sacred Body by the scourges, the thorns, the nails, and the lance. The immaculate bosom of Our Lady is then incomparably more worthy of honour than the ancient ark which prefigured it.

O Most Holy and Most Happy Lady, raised in Paradise to the highest degree of beatitude and happiness! we beg you to have compassion on us who groan in the desert of this world. You are in the abundance of delights, and we in the abyss of miseries; obtain for us strength to endure our tribulations virtuously, always leaning on your Beloved Son, the only pledge of our hopes and remedy of our evils. O Glorious Virgin, pray for the Church, assist the Holy Father, the Prelates, Bishops, and all Superiors; and assist England especially, which by your devoted servant St. Edward, was consecrated to you as your dowry: *Dota Mariæ*. (Translator.)

You are the Mother of Jesus, Who has deigned to become our Brother, and hence you are our Mother; why, then, shall we not cast ourselves into your arms with perfect confidence, invoking your maternal love and imitating your virtues? O God, what a blessing for us to be sons of such a Mother! If we love and serve her with a truly filial love, she will enrich us with her favours. And, meanwhile, let us present her with the flowers of every virtue: but, above all, with the lily of purity, the rose of ardent charity, and the violets of holy humility and simplicity. She loves nothing so much as hearts deepened by humility, opened by simplicity, and enlarged by charity; and she prefers to be in the company of souls near the manger and at the foot of the Cross; that is, with the poor and the afflicted, in order to succour and console them.

SPIRITUAL FLOWERS

Mary is like a lily amidst thorns: she loves and suffers at the same time. When the thorns are blown about by the wind, they tear the lily on all sides; but it revenges itself by causing to exhale, through the apertures of its wounds, a sweet fragrance, which perfumes the thorns that have so cruelly wounded it. In imitation of Mary, figured by the lily amidst thorns, let your only revenge for your afflictions be to increase your love for those who are the cause of your pains.—*Père Avrillion.*

Mary is compared to the white lily, on account of her innocence and exemption from all sin; and as the lily is beautiful amongst the thorns where it has sprung up, so was Mary distinguished amidst the women of Judea. The lily loses nothing of its whiteness, although amongst thorns, and the august Virgin, tortured in the

Person of her Son, by the Jewish Deicides, preserved the innocency of her soul and the purity of her heart, rendering good for evil.—*St. Francis de Sales.*

Mary is that most beautiful and lofty cedar, from which God detached the finest branch, to transplant it on Calvary.—*The same.*

Lose not sight of eternity, and the adversities of this life will not trouble you.—*The same.*

EXAMPLE

The 'Regina Cœli'

Baronius and St. Gregory of Nyssa relate that in the year 690 the city of Rome was in danger of becoming a desert, on account of the number of persons who became victims to a terrible pestilence. St. Gregory, surnamed the Great, successor to Pope Gelasius II., who had fallen a victim to this disease, saw that all human precautions and resources were of no avail, and he resolved to have recourse to the Mother of God. He gave orders that the picture of the Most Holy Virgin—which is believed to have been painted by St. Luke—should be carried in a general procession of all the Clergy and laity, as far as Santa Maria Maggiore.

The violence of the plague was such that eighty persons perished during the procession; but before its termination an Angel was seen in human form above Adrian's Tower (called afterwards the Castle of St. Angelo, in memory of this event), sheathing a sword tinged with blood, as in the time of David; and from that moment the pestilence completely ceased. At the same time many voices were heard in the air, singing: *Regina cœli, lætare, alleluia; quia quem meruisti portare, alleluia; resurrexit sicut dixit, alleluia*—'Rejoice, O Queen of Heaven, for He Whom you deserved to bear has risen, as He said, from the grave; God be praised.' The Holy Pontiff immediately added: *Ora pro nobis Deum, alleluia*—'Pray to God for us, God be praised.'

This having occurred at Easter, the Church from that time ordered all the Clergy and faithful to recite this Antiphon during Paschal season.

Prayer.—Oh! most desolate of Mothers! what a sword has pierced your Heart! All the blows which wounded your Son Jesus fell upon you. By His pains you were tortured, by His wounds you were torn. His last adieu renewed all your sorrows; but when He breathed His last sigh with what anguish was your heart oppressed, O Mother of love and of sorrow! Obtain, I beg of you, that I may follow your example in loving and suffering! Yes, Queen of Martyrs, let me share your martyrdom. Love gave you the Cross, let the Cross fill my heart with love; and if, to enable me to love, it be necessary that I suffer and die, obtain for me this grace, that I may love all that comes to me from God, whether it be sorrows, afflictions, or death. Amen.

Aspiration.—Pray for me, O Queen of Martyrs!

Practice.—When you are tempted to complain, or to be impatient under opposition, reflect upon Mary at the foot of the Cross.

Twenty-Sixth Day

Mary After the Ascension of Christ

God placed two beautiful luminaries in the heavens on the fourth day of the Creation; one called the *greater*, the other the *lesser light*; the former to rule over the day, the latter, over the night. Although God decreed that darkness should succeed the day, He, the increated Light, would not allow the night to be entirely deprived of light. When, in His Providence, He wished to create the spiritual world in His Church, He placed in it, as in a Divine firmament, two great luminaries. The greatest is Jesus Christ, Our Saviour and Master—an abyss of light, and the source of splendour, the true Sun of Justice; the lesser luminary is the Most Holy Mother of this Divine Saviour; a most glorious Mother, resplendent and beautiful as the moon.

The Son of God came down upon earth, like the sun upon our atmosphere, to clothe Himself with our humanity, and formed our light and day; a most longed-for day, which lasted about thirty-three years, during which time He illumined the Church with the splendour of His miracles, His example and His doctrine. But the hour having at last arrived when this precious Sun was to set and cast Its rays over the other hemisphere—that is, heaven—what else could remain on earth but darkness and obscurity? And, in fact, night quickly spread around—the night of the many persecutions raised against the Apostles. But that its darkness might be more tolerable, it also had its luminary in the person of the Most Holy Virgin, who remained with the disciples and the faithful, after the Ascension of her Divine Son. This we learn from St. Luke: the Most Holy Mary was with the disciples in the upper room on the day of Pentecost, and persevered with them in communion and prayer.

Jesus Christ would leave her still in the world: firstly, that as a luminary she might be the comfort of the faithful immersed in the night of tribulations; secondly, that by surviving her Divine Son she might acquire greater merit, so that it might be truly said of her—many daughters have gathered riches, you have surpassed them all; thirdly, that her presence might be a convincing proof against the heresy that arose after the Ascension of Our Lord, which held that He had not taken a natural Body but one merely in appearance. Thus, even in her lifetime, were verified in her regard the words of Holy Church, 'You, august Virgin, have destroyed all heresies.'

The Most Holy Virgin lived after the Ascension of her Divine Son until she reached the age of sixty-three; and thus this mystic Ark of the new Covenant dwelt under tents in the desert of this world.

Our Divine Lord, wished that His Most Holy Mother should, after having been an example to virgins and to mothers, become the model of widows by her modesty and her love for the hidden life. Widows may be compared to the little lowly violet, which has no brilliancy in its colour but has a scent which, without being too strong, is marvellously sweet. Oh, what a beautiful flower in the Church is the Christian widow! Lowly, through humility, and without splendour in the eyes of the world, since she flies from it; she is unable to meet the gaze of men when her heart no longer desires their love.

The Apostle St. Paul orders his disciple St. Timothy, to honour those *who are widows indeed;* that is, those who are so in heart and mind. 'Blessed,' says Our Lord, 'are the pure of heart and poor in spirit.'

Widows in spirit and in desire are deserving of the highest esteem; for what means the word 'widow' but need and destitution. Honour, then, be rendered to those who are such in mind and heart, for they are humble and their Protector is the Lord!

SPIRITUAL FLOWERS

Let it be your desire to see God, your fear to lose Him, your sorrow not yet to possess Him, and your joy to do everything that can lead you to Him; you will then live in the abundance of peace.—*St. Teresa.*

Remember that you have but one soul; that you will die but once; that you have but one life, and that a very short one; but one glory, and that eternal; your heart will then detach itself from everything.—*The same.*

The soul that loves God lives more in the next world than in this; because the soul lives more in the object of its love than in the subject which it animates.—*St. John of the Cross.*

The true widow of the Church is a little March violet. By her devotion she spreads a sweet perfume. She usually keeps herself hidden under the leaves of her abjection, and her mortification is seen by her quiet, modest demeanour.—*St. Francis de Sales.*

EXAMPLE

A Courageous Son of Mary

The Saints are accustomed to say 'My Mother' when speaking of the Blessed Virgin Mary; and some time ago, under the influence of this idea, a touching scene took place. A countryman was at Leipsic, a town which may be called the heart of Protestantism, where he entered by mistake the hall of a university, in which some Lutheran Doctors were disputing upon religion. He was recognised as a fervent Catholic, by a medal attached to his rosary hanging from his pocket; and he soon became the object of the bitter derision of the Lutherans.

The good man, without being disconcerted, took a dollar from his old purse, and, throwing it on the table where the Doctors were seated, exclaimed, 'Well, then, who will bet with me which of us is the most learned in matters of religion?'

The president laid down his piece of money; and then casting a glance of contempt upon the peasant's rosary, said to him, 'What is the name of the Mother of God?' The pious peasant replied, in a most respectful tone of voice, 'Her name is Mary.' Then, quickly turning to the Doctor, he said, 'Tell me the name of *my* Mother.'

This question contained a mystery; a Catholic would have penetrated it. and would have replied, 'She is called Mary.' However, the Protestant Doctor was not sufficiently instructed to understand it. He remained silent, filled with spite at the ingenious and pious trick of the countryman, who, judging that he had come off victor, took up the two pieces of money, and said, with admirable calmness, 'Gentlemen, when you dispute again upon religion, I beg of you to let me know.' He then retired; and the lesson was as perfect as it was well merited.

Prayer.—O Mary, my Sovereign! O Mother of my Saviour! You are blessed amongst all women, pure amongst all virgins, the Queen of all creatures. All nations call you Blessed. Let me exalt your greatness as much as it is possible for me to exalt it, and love you, as much as I can love you. May I call upon you continually and contribute to make you honoured, as far as I am able. I should wish to see the whole universe prostrate at your feet, and all hearts burning with your love, that they may all love your Divine Son, as you loved Him in this world, and will love Him for all eternity. I earnestly entreat this grace, O my Mother, although I acknowledge and confess myself unworthy to obtain it.

Aspiration.—O Holy Virgin, enable me to speak of your greatness.

Practice.—Examine if the virtues of Mary are to you as that lesser luminary in whose light you walk on in the way that leads to Paradise.

Twenty-Seventh Day

Mary in the Upper Room at Jerusalem

The Eternal Father bestowed an incomparable gift upon the world when He gave it His Only Son. Jesus Christ Himself said: 'God hath so loved the world as to give it His Only Son;' and St. Paul exclaims: 'How has He not with Him given us all things?'—*Quomodo non etiam omnia cum illo nobis donavit?*

Almighty God, in the ancient Law, had bestowed an infinity of blessings upon His chosen people; but they were given according to measure. In the Law of Grace, however, He had no sooner seen His Beloved Son ascended into heaven than He opened His Hands to pour forth His graces and gifts upon all the faithful, according to the prophecy of Joel, that *supra omnem carnem*—'over all men' would He diffuse His Holy Spirit.

If we desire to receive this Divine Spirit, let us beg Our Lord to bestow Him upon us through the merits of his Most Holy Mother, the glorious Virgin Mary, and through the love He bore to her; and we shall thus, like the Apostles, be with *Mary the Mother of Jesus*. We shall never understand how necessary is this condition. St. Elizabeth had no sooner spoken to the Most Holy Virgin than she was immediately, says St. Luke, 'filled with the Holy Ghost.' Nor is this a subject of wonder, because Mary is the Spouse of the Holy Ghost, the Daughter of the Eternal Father, and the Mother of the Eternal Son.

The Evangelist St. Luke, by observing that men and women were assembled in the room, admonishes us that we must all hope to receive the Holy Ghost; but he mentions in particular the presence of *Mary the Mother of Jesus*, to insinuate that she was there as the Queen of the Apostles. How mistaken, then, are those who say that we honour the Most Holy Virgin too much! This august Virgin, it is true, had already received the Holy Spirit and the fulness of grace in the Annunciation, but in the upper room she received a great superabundance of grace.

Whoever, then, desires to receive the Holy Ghost, let him unite himself to Mary; because he who separates himself from her, does not gather but scatters. Let us serve her, honour her, that He Who comes into our hearts, by her mediation, may also receive us by the same mediation.

To conclude, we may learn a very useful lesson from the words of St. Luke about the Disciples when they had received the Holy Ghost: 'All spoke in divers tongues according as the Holy Ghost gave them to speak'—*Prout Spiritus Sanctus dabat eloqui illis;* that is, that though all spoke, yet they did not speak in the same manner. The Apostles preached the new Law; and those who did not preach publicly, animated one another to praise and magnify the Lord. Let us, however, understand that there is an efficacious method of speaking without even uttering a word, and it is by the good example which we give to our neighbour.

David says: 'The heavens declare the glory of God. Day unto day uttereth speech, and night unto night showeth knowledge.' These words signify that the beauty of the heavens invites men to admire the magnificence of the Creator. Indeed, when on a clear night we contemplate the beauty of the heavens, we do not feel less animated to admire and adore the Omnipotence and Wisdom of God, Who has studded it with such beautiful stars, than when we observe the inaccessible light of the sun in its full meridian splendour. What conclusion are we to draw from all this but that we, who are something more than all the rest of creation (since all things were made for us, and not we for them), should, by our good example, announce the glory of God more perfectly than the heavens and the stars. Good example is a silent but a most efficacious influence. In this manner we can all preach, although we have not all received the gift of tongues. Is it a less wonder to see a soul adorned with many sublime virtues than to see the heavens decorated with magnificent stars? How much, my God, do I need the Spirit of strength when I feel myself so weak and infirm! However, I glory in my infirmity *that the Power of my God may dwell in me*. Let us glory in our weakness, which makes us fitting receptacles of the Power of God. May He grant that this sacred fire, which can entirely change us into Him, may transform our hearts into His pure Love, that we may be all love and not lovers only. May He grant me also to receive and make good use of the gift of understanding, that my mind may be more enlightened to penetrate clearly the sacred mysteries of our holy Faith; for this understanding has a wonderful power to subjugate the will to the service of Him Whom it recognises to be so good and so worthy of love, Yet, as true love is active, we need counsel, that we may be able to discern how to exercise this love; and then our soul is excellently endowed with the sacred gifts of Heaven.

May the Holy Spirit, Who favours us with His gifts, form our whole consolation, and be eternally adored by my mind and by my heart! May He be always our wisdom and our understanding, our counsel and our fortitude, our knowledge and our piety, and fill us with the spirit of the fear of the Lord.

SPIRITUAL FLOWERS

Mary is the root of Jesse, upon whom the Holy Spirit rested. The Son of the Virgin is the flower thereof; a red and white flower, chosen amongst thousands—the flower upon which the Angels gaze with continuous desire; a flower whose fragrance renews life; a flower of everlasting bloom, whose beauty is incorruptible, and whose glory will never fade.—*St. Bernard.*

Mary is the root of that beautiful flower upon which the Holy Spirit rests with the fulness of His gifts. Whoever then desires to obtain the seven gifts of the Holy Ghost, must seek the flower upon the stem; because we reach the flower through the stem, and through the flower we find the Holy Spirit, Who thereon reposes. Let us go to Jesus, through Mary;

and by means of Jesus, we find the grace of the Holy Spirit.—*St. Bonaventure.*

Give your soul to God a thousand times in the day; fix your interior eyes upon His sweetness, in imitation of Mary; place Him upon your breast as a delicious nosegay, and make every possible effort to excite within you an impassioned love for this Divine Spouse.—*St. Francis de Sales.*

There is no doubt that he who perfumes the world by the odour of his good example, thus teaching others the way of justice, will one day shine in eternity as a most splendid star in the firmament.—*The same.*

EXAMPLE

The Prayer 'Memorare'

St. Francis de Sales had received, in his youth, a miraculous proof of the protection of Mary. Being assaulted by a violent temptation to believe himself reprobated by God, he experienced such anguish that he compared it to the sorrows of death and the torments of hell. After a month passed in these desolating trials, earnestly desiring to be delivered from them, he humbly prostrated himself before a statue of the Blessed Virgin, and with great confidence recited the *Memorare*, beseeching Our Lady to obtain from her Divine Son that, if he should ever have the misfortune of being eternally separated from his God, he might at least love Him during the present lifetime with all his powers.

The Most Holy Virgin could not be deaf to such a petition, and Francis quickly recovered the peace of heart he had lost. From that time he had the greatest confidence in this prayer, and recited it in every difficult undertaking, and recommended it warmly to all whom he directed.

'I remember,' says the Bishop of Belley, 'to have learnt this prayer from him, and in order to impress it more deeply in my heart, and to make use of it in all my afflictions, I wrote it down at the beginning of my breviary. I know, moreover, that he commended it much to the Nuns of the Visitation. He wished it to be repeated above all in times of great temptations, because the Mother of God is as terrible to the enemy as an army in battle array; the blessed fruit of her womb having crushed the head of the infernal serpent.'

It is generally believed that St. Bernard was the author of this prayer.

Prayer to ask for the Seven Gifts of the Holy Ghost.—August Spouse of the Holy Ghost, Most Holy Virgin Mary, the inexhaustible source of grace, deign to obtain for me from your Divine Spouse the gift of Wisdom, which may detach me from the goods of the world, and make me love those of heaven; the gift of Understanding, which may teach me my duties; the gift of Counsel, which may enlighten me in the way of salvation; the gift of Fortitude, which may sustain my weakness; the gift of Knowledge, which may teach me the eternal truths; the gift of Piety, which may render the service of God sweet to me; and the gift of Fear, which may inspire me with a holy respect and tender love towards the God of infinite mercy. Ah! my continued resistance to the inspirations of the Holy Spirit have rendered me unworthy of such a benefit, but, aided by your prayers, I confidently hope to obtain from the author of *every perfect gift* the graces that are necessary to live holily in this life, and thus one day attain to the eternal beatitude of heaven. Amen.

Aspiration.—Pray for me, O Spouse of the Holy Ghost.

Practice.—Accustom yourself in every difficulty to say at once: *O Mother of Good Counsel, inspire me!*

Twenty-Eighth Day

How Precious in the Sight of God Was the Death of Mary

According to the common opinion of the Doctors of the Church, when the Blessed Virgin Mary had attained the age of sixty-three she died, or rather, she slept the sleep of death. But how is it, some will say, that Our Lord, Who loved His Holy Mother so tenderly, did not grant her the privilege of exemption from death, since death is the wages of sin, and she had never sinned? How contrary are such thoughts to those of God, and how far removed are such judgments from His! We know that death became precious when Our Lord permitted that its blow should fall upon Him, on the Tree of the Cross. Certainly, the Most Holy Virgin thought it no advantage or privilege not to die, but she always desired death, for she saw it lovingly embraced by her Divine Son. He had rendered it so sweet and desirable that the Angels would consider themselves most fortunate to be able to die, and the Saints looked upon it as a happiness, and therefore experienced great consolation in it. Our adorable Saviour, who is Life

Itself, gave life to death by His own death, so that to those who die in the grace of God, it is the beginning of eternal life.

Consider this Queen, dying of a fever, that was sweeter to her than health, because it was the fever of Divine love, which, by burning up her heart, consumed it so completely as to open to her soul the way by which it flew into the arms of her Divine Son.

All the Saints die in the habit of holy Love; but some amongst them die in the exercise of this Divine love; others, on account of it, as the Martyrs; and others, by its power. But the most sublime degree of holy love is to die of love itself; and this occurs when the soul is so inflamed by charity that it can no longer be detained by the bonds of the flesh.

If it be true that such as is *the life of a man such will be his death*, what else can have been the death of the Most Holy Virgin but the death of love? This is certain; because she who is called in the language of Sacred Scripture, the *Mother of fair Love* could only die the death of love. We read not of ecstasies and raptures in the life of Our Lady, and for this reason, that they were continual. She loved God with so tender, so strong, and so ardent a love, at the same time so tranquilly, and with so much peace, that although her love went on increasing, the increase was not impetuous, but she continually, and almost imperceptibly, hastened towards this so greatly desired union of her soul with God, like a river that calmly flows to the ocean.

The hour having then arrived when the Most Holy Virgin was to leave the earth, Divine Love separated her soul from her body, and incomparably pure as it was, it flew directly to heaven. Ah! what obstacle could detain her whom the Celestial Spouse calls 'His beloved, all fair and without spot'? Our imperfections and the stains of our sins are the only obstacle to our entrance into heaven at the moment of our death; and it is these that are the origin of the flames of Purgatory.

The Saints are ever burning with the fire of Divine love; and by their exemplary lives spread a continual odour of sanctity in the presence of men and of God. This odour is incomparably increased at their death; hence the Prophet says: 'Precious in the sight of the Lord is the death of the Saints.'

If, then, the Saints are odoriferous and burning lamps, what shall we say of the Most Holy Virgin, whose perfection immeasurably surpassed that of all the Saints united together? If in life she was a Burning Lamp, fed with the perfumed oil of every virtue, what a fragrance must she have exhaled at the hour of her death! So great was this fragrance that young virgins, as we read in the Canticles, were attracted by it: 'We will run after thee to the odour of thy perfumes,' 'the young maidens have loved thee.'

SPIRITUAL FLOWERS

The soul of Mary was released from her body as naturally as fragrance sent from a flower and as the ripe fruit falls from the tree.—*St. Francis de Sales.*

As the palm conceals its flower until the heat of the sun causes it to expand, so the just soul conceals the flowers of its virtue by humility, until Our Lord, by calling her to Paradise, gives the highest degree of perfection to her love.—*The same.*

The thought of death is not sad for a soul who loves God, because it is the beginning of her eternal happiness.—*St. John of the Cross.*

O Death, most beautiful Death! wherefore shall we fear thee, if in thee is found life? He alone should fear thee who has persevered in sin until his last breath.—*St. Teresa.*

EXAMPLE

Letters Addressed to the Most Holy Virgin

Persons filled with lively faith often write letters to the Blessed Virgin Mary, placing them at the feet of her image, or upon their heart, on some solemn occasion; and this practice is very dear to her,

It is no new practice: for we see, from the Sacred Books and the history of the Church, that the most remarkable men made use of it to obtain some special grace. King Ezechias carried into the Temple the insulting letter addressed to him by Zennacherib, and laid it on the Altar as if to invite Almighty God to read it, and his prayer was heard, as we read in the Fourth Book of Kings.

The Emperor Theodosius, about to fight against Eugenius, wrote to St. Ambrose, to beg him to recommend the expedition to the God of armies. The Saint, during Mass, took the letter into his hands, and presented it to God. The result of the battle is well known.

When the Angelic Doctor, St. Thomas, met with some difficult passage in Holy Scripture, he wrote down the difficulty and placed it on his heart when he went to celebrate Mass, and the difficulties vanished.

Our Lord looks upon prayers addressed to the Blessed Virgin and to the Saints as though they were made to Himself. If we wish to obtain some grace, let us write a letter to Mary, and place it upon our heart before we approach Holy Communion. St. Stanislaus Kostka, desired to die on the Eve of the Assumption, that he might assist at its celebration in heaven. He wrote a letter to Our Blessed Lady for this purpose, and, on the feast of St. Lawrence, placed it on the Altar, asking the Saint to present it to the Queen of Heaven. The same day he was attacked by a most burning fever, and after four days went to celebrate the feast of his dear Mother Mary in heaven.

Prayer (of St. Alphonsus Liguori to obtain a happy death).—O Mary! what will be my death? When I think of the moment which is to decide my eternal destiny, I fear and tremble at the sight of my sins. O Mother, full of goodness, the Blood of Jesus Christ and your patronage are alone my hope. Ah, console me in that terrible moment, O Consoler of the afflicted! If I am now tormented by remorse for my offences, through the uncertainty of pardon, the danger of falling again, and the judgments of God, what will it be at that moment? I am lost if you do not fly to my relief.

O my sovereign Lady, obtain for me, before my death, lively sorrow for sin, true amendment, and entire fidelity to God; and may I at that moment invoke you more frequently, that I may not despair at the sight of my sins. Pardon me my rashness, O my Queen; but I beg you also to come yourself to console me by your presence, You have granted this favour to so many of your servants, and why should not I also hope for it? It is true I do not merit it; but I love you, O Mary, and confide in you. I expect then your presence and assistance, that I may go forth from this world loving God, and you also, my Holy Mother, and never cease to love you through all eternity. Amen.

Aspiration.—Do not abandon me at the hour of my death, O my Most Holy Mother!

Practice.—Spend this day as if it were the last of your life.

Twenty-Ninth Day

Mary, like Jesus, Dies of Divine Love

Our Lady died of Divine love, like her adorable Son. The foundation of this belief is, that having but one life with her Divine Son, she could have but one and the same death. In reality, they were two distinct persons; but they had one heart, one soul, one mind, one life!

If this was said of the first Christians; if Jesus Christ lived in St. Paul, because his spirit was dead in the Heart of his Saviour, with much greater truth could it be said that Jesus Christ and His Most Holy Mother had but one heart and one soul, and, consequently, one life; for there never was a Mother so loving or so much loved; and the quality of Mother and only Son gives us the idea of all that is most perfect and most excellent in love.

If the Apostle St. Paul could say that he had no other life than that of his Divine Master, with greater reason could Mary, the Mother of this amiable Master, say: 'I have no other life than that of my Divine Son:

He lives in me and I in Him.' And having lived the life of her Son, she must have died the death of her Son. This death was prophesied to her, by holy Simeon, in these words: 'Thy own soul a sword shall pierce.'

Three kinds of swords can pierce the soul: the first, the sword of the Word of God, which, in the saying of the Apostle, 'is more penetrating than a two-edged sword'; the second, the sword of suffering and sorrow, according to the prophecy of Simeon; and the third, the sword of Divine Love, of which Jesus Christ speaks: 'I came not to bring peace, but the sword.' Now, the soul of Our Lady was pierced by all these three kinds of swords in the death of her Son.

When a heavy blow falls upon an object, everything near it feels its effects. Thus, although the body of the Most Holy Virgin was not united to that of her Divine Son in His Passion, yet, her soul being inseparably united to Him, it follows that all the blows with which His Blessed Body was bruised wounded her soul.

Love causes us to feel the afflictions of those we love, as we see in St. Paul, who was weak with the weak, afflicted with those in tribulation; and yet the soul of this Apostle certainly was not so closely united to the faithful as the soul of Our Lady to the soul and body of Jesus. No wonder, then, that the thorns, the nails and lance, which pierced the head, hands, feet and side of Our Lord, pierced also through and through the soul of His Mother.

Truly may we exclaim: O Most Holy Virgin! how deeply was your soul pierced by the love, the suffering, and the words of your Son! And, oh, how deep a wound love gave you, when you saw the Son, Who loved you so much, and Who possessed all the affections of your heart, expiring through love! How bitterly did sorrow, too, wound your soul, when you saw the sufferings that led your only Son to death! And, as for His words, like a strong wind they inflamed your love, excited your sorrow, and almost engulfed the vessel of your heart in an ocean of grief.

Love caused Mary to be penetrated with sorrow; and the sufferings of her Son were expressed in words that pierced her heart like darts. And, as a stag wounded by the hunter, flees with the arrow fixed in the wound, to die afar off, and sometimes, long after it has received the blow; so Our Lady, wounded by the sword of sorrow in the Passion of her Son upon Calvary, survived the wound she had received many years, but at last it caused her death. Oh, loving wound! Oh, sword of charity! how dear and beloved wast thou to the tender heart which thou didst pierce!

The philosopher Aristotle narrates that when the wild goats of Candia are wounded by a dart, they have recourse to the herb dittany, and by means of this plant the dart comes out of the wound. Ah! who is there that does not feel his heart wounded by the thought of the Passion of Jesus Christ, contemplating Him scourged, crowned with thorns and crucified? But, alas! I scarcely dare to say it: the greater number who are pierced by this dart run quickly, like those goats, to the dittany of worldly consolations in order to remove from their heart the wound of Divine love. The Blessed Virgin, on the contrary, zealously preserved this dart, and it formed all her glory and her triumph.

SPIRITUAL FLOWERS

Thorns are the flowers of Calvary, and sufferings the flowers of the Cross; and this is the support sought for by the languishing love of Mary.—*Bossuet.*

Oh how sweet will death be to the Christian who has done penance for his sins during life! He will pass instantly to the ineffable joys of Paradise.—*St. Teresa.*

Mystical death is accompanied by a sweetness and a satisfaction a thousand times greater than the full life of the senses.—*P. Milley.*

The more a soul knows the perfections of God, the more does the desire to see Him increase within itself.—*St. John of the Cross.*

The happiness of dying without regret well repays us for living without pleasures.—*The same.*

EXAMPLE

The Fourteen Joys of the Most Holy Virgin

St. Thomas of Canterbury had the pious custom of reciting seven *Ave Marias* every day in honour of the Seven Joys of Our Lady upon earth: the Annunciation, the Visitation, the Birth of Our Lord, the Epiphany, the Finding in the Temple, the Resurrection, and the Ascension. One day the Blessed Virgin appeared to him, and said: 'Thy devotion, Thomas, is very pleasing to me; but why dost thou commemorate only the joys I experienced whilst on earth? Henceforth, be mindful also of those that I enjoy in heaven; I assure thee that I will console and present to my Son, at the hour of their death, all those who during life shall have honoured the latter, as well as the former joys.' The holy Archbishop, filled with consolation at these words, exclaimed: 'But how can I do so, Most Holy Virgin, when I know not these joys?' The august Mother of God then taught the Saint to recite seven *Ave Marias* in honour of the following joys: the honour that the Most Holy Trinity conferred upon her above all creatures; the excellence of her Virginity, which raised her above the Angels and the Saints; the splendour of her glory, which illuminates heaven; the veneration paid to her by the Blessed, on account of her dignity of Mother of God; her power with her Divine Son in our behalf; the graces with which she was enriched when on earth, and the reward reserved in heaven for those who are devout to her during life; finally, her accidental glory, which will continually increase until the Day of Judgment.

Many Saints have practised this devotion with fruit, and a great number of the devoted servants of Mary have made use of it to honour their august Mother.

Prayer of St. Alfonso Maria di Liguori.—Mary! I acknowledge that you are the most beautiful, the most holy, and most amiable of all creatures. Ah! would that all knew you, O Holy Virgin, and loved you as you deserve. I rejoice that you are so revered by all the

Blessed in heaven, and by so many faithful souls on earth, but especially that you are so much loved by God. Most amiable Queen! I also love you, miserable sinner that I am, and I desire to love you more; obtain for me, then, this love, O my dear Mother, because it is a sign of predestination. I know that you will help me, and by your help I shall conquer, if I cease not to recommend myself to you. But I fear that I may not always invoke you in occasions of danger; succour me then always, O Mary, my good Mother, and never permit me to offend my God. Amen.

Aspiration.—In your love do I wish to live and die, my Blessed Mother!

Practice.—Offer an act of mortification to God, through the Blessed Virgin, for those who are to die this day.

Thirtieth Day

The Death of Mary Was Sweet and Tranquil

As the peaceful morning dawns, not by fits and starts, but steadily and gradually, so that its progress is scarcely perceptible, so did Divine love increase in the heart of Our Lady, the glorious Virgin Mary. Her progress in charity was tranquil, uniform and uninterrupted, so that she continually pursued her course towards the Divinity Whom she loved.

Consider that love is, in its nature, calm, tranquil, and full of sweetness, and becomes violent only when it meets with some opposition. But if its dominion in a soul be undisputed, and if nothing oppose its progress, then it works steadily and gains its victories with ease. We may understand, then, how the heart of the Mother of pure Love experienced all its power, without any impetuous movement, for in her there was no resistance to overcome.

Observe the course of great rivers: when the bed is not level and the current is encumbered with masses of rock, the waters splash and foam, and roll back again with a great noise; but when the bed is smooth the waters flow on placidly and without effort. Such is the case with holy love, when it meets with obstacles,—and where does it not find them? It is constrained to struggle with a kind of violence against the human inclinations that oppose it; to use force, and make great efforts in order to bend the will, to remove impediments, and to open a passage for itself to the heart it seeks to possess. In the Blessed Virgin, however, everything favoured and seconded the attractions of grace and of Divine love, and although her love was incomparably greater than that of any other creature, it continually went on increasing with the greatest calm and sweetness.

If iron were not held down by its weight it would find no obstacle to the continued attraction of the magnet, and its strong and even motion would continually increase in proportion as the iron and magnet drew nearer to each other. Thus it was with the Most Holy Virgin at her death. As there was nothing in her that could impede the action of Divine love, she became more and more closely united to her adorable Son through sweet ecstasies, until she became, so to speak, immersed in the bosom of His goodness; and thus, without even knowing it, she quitted her body and was reunited to her Divine Son in heaven.

It was fitting that as love had produced the sorrows of death in this Divine Mother at the foot of the Cross, so death should in its turn, produce the sovereign delights of love. Ah! may this Most Holy Virgin obtain for us, by her prayers, grace to live in holy love, and may it alone be the object of all our desires, and of all the affections of our hearts!

SPIRITUAL FLOWERS

St. Gregory says that the pomegranate, by its bright red colour, its beautiful corona, and numerous seeds so well arranged, sweetly represents charity. Charity is red, by the ardour with which it burns for God, is adorned with the variety of every virtue, and obtains and wears for ever the crown of eternal rewards.—*St. Francis de Sales.*

Bees never sting so sharply as when they are themselves mortally wounded. How can we fail to be wounded with love for our adorable Saviour, when we contemplate Him wounded for us, even unto death and the death of the Cross; to be wounded, I say, with a wound the more painfully loving, as His was more lovingly painful; nor can we ever love Him as much as His death and His love merit.—*The same.*

EXAMPLE

Novenas in Honour of the Blessed Virgin

In the various tribulations of life, in great afflictions, dangers and temptations, when we require special assistance from God, an almost certain means to obtain it is to make a Novena in honour of the Most Blessed Virgin Mary. How many souls have been heard by God, by having had recourse to the Most Holy Virgin through a Novena!

The Children of Mary apply themselves with special devotion and fervent piety to the celebration of her festivals, and, in return, the Blessed Virgin obtains for them an abundance of heavenly blessings. St. Gertrude saw one day a great number of souls under the mantle of Mary, guarded by her with warm affection, and she understood that they had prepared themselves, by devout exercises of piety, for celebrating the Feast of the Assumption of Our Lady.

Prayer.—O Queen of Paradise! raised above all the heavenly choirs, seated at the right hand of your Divine Son, I prostrate myself at your feet, miserable sinner that I am, and conjure you to cast upon me those eyes of mercy which bring grace and the friendship of Almighty God wherever they are turned. Observe, O Most Holy Mary, in how many dangers I am of losing my soul, and shall always be as long as I am on earth; but I place all my hopes in you. I love you, my Mother, with all my heart, and wish to love you for ever. Ah! pray to your Divine Son for me; tell Him to protect me, and He will assuredly have compassion on my poor soul. O my sweetest and most compassionate Mother, in this hope do I rest, and wish also to live and die. Amen.

Aspiration.—O Mary! love gave you the Cross! May the Cross give us love!

Practice.—Examine what would give you most fear if you were going to die now, and begin earnestly to amend.

Thirty-First Day

The Resurrection and Assumption of the Blessed Virgin

There can be no doubt whatever that Our Lord fulfilled towards Mary the precept which He gave in general to all children to honour their parents. Indeed, where is the son who would not raise his mother from the grave to lead her to Paradise, if he had it in his power? The great triumph of the Assumption of the Blessed Virgin is celebrated by all the Saints, and by the whole Church Militant.

After the Ark of the Covenant had dwelt for a long period under tents and pavilions, King Solomon ordered it to be placed in the marvellous Temple he had prepared for it. The joy of the Hebrews on that occasion was so great that the blood of the sacrifices flowed through the streets of Jerusalem; the air was filled with clouds of incense, and the houses and public squares resounded with harmonious music.

But, O God! if the solemnity of the reception of the Ark was so great, what must have been that of the Most Glorious Virgin, Mother of the Son of God, the true Ark of the New Covenant, upon the day of her Assumption! O incomprehensible joy! festival of wonders! which makes all devout souls who are the true daughters of Jerusalem, exclaim: 'Who is she that goeth up from the desert leaning upon her Beloved?' The entrance of the Most Blessed Virgin into heaven was the most magnificent that ever could or can be witnessed after that of Jesus Christ. She ascends from the desert of this lower world, so perfumed with spiritual gifts that, except in the Person of her Divine Son, she has no equal in heaven. The Queen of Saba, coming to Jerusalem to have a proof of the wisdom of Solomon, brought with her a great quantity of perfumes, gold, and precious stones. But, when the Most Holy Virgin entered heaven, she carried with her such an amount of the pure gold of charity, so much perfume of devotion and of virtue, and so many precious gems of patience and of suffering, that we can safely say no one ever had so great an accumulation of merits to offer her Divine Son! Yes, indeed, she abounded in delights, because during her life on earth she had abounded in good works and in sufferings.

We may say that, in one sense, the Assumption of Our Lady was even more glorious than the Ascension of Jesus Christ; because the Angels only were present at the Ascension, whilst at the Assumption of Our Lady the King of Angels Himself attended her.

What a triumph was it for Heaven, and what a consolation for earth! Ah, let us in spirit dwell and live in heaven, because there is our treasure and our life. O my God! how beautiful is heaven now that its sun is Our Blessed Saviour, and His bosom is the Source of Love, where the Blessed drink and quench their thirst! If we look up there, we shall see our names written in characters of Love, which can be read only by Love, and engraved only by Love. O God! and will my name also be there? Let me trust so; because although my heart burns not with ardent Charity, it has, however, its desire and its principle, and bears written upon it the Sacred Name of Jesus, which I hope nothing will be able to cancel. O what a joy for us when we shall see those characters denoting our eternal happiness! As for me, although those eternal blessings occupy all my desires and affections, yet all Paradise would be nothing to me if I did not find there the never-ending Love of the Eternal God, Who lives and reigns for ever and ever.

Let us bear in mind that Jesus Christ looks upon us from heaven, and sweetly invites us to come and enjoy the delights of His goodness and the abundance of His love. The Most Holy Virgin also invites us as a Mother, saying to each of us: 'Courage, my child; despise not the ardent desires of my Son, and my sighs and petitions for thy salvation.' And yet, how often have we not preferred the miserable vanities and bitter pleasures of earth to those incomparable joys! Ah, faithful souls; let us henceforth accept the favours which the Most Holy Virgin and the Saints offer us. Let us promise them to walk quickly on towards heaven; and let us take hold of the hand of our good Angel-guardian, that we may never again stumble, but happily reach the gates of a blessed eternity.

SPIRITUAL FLOWERS

The qualities of the material rose vividly represent the attributes of Mary, the Mystical Rose. The perfume of the rose signifies the joys of the Most Blessed Virgin; its thorns represent to us her sorrows; and the beauty of its colour her glory in heaven.

Mary is the beautiful Lily who looks down from her high throne upon all other flowers, and sees them inferior to herself.—*St. John Damascen.*

The difference between material and spiritual rose-trees is this, that in the former, the roses fade and the thorns remain; whilst, in the latter, the thorns pass away and the roses remain.—*St. Francis de Sales.*

EXAMPLE

The Novena of St. Gertrude to the Blessed Virgin

St. Gertrude, a Benedictine nun, cherished a great devotion to the Most Blessed Virgin. On the eve of the Annunciation she had a vision, in which she seemed to see her religious Sisters offering nosegays of sweet flowers to Our Lady. These were collected by Our Lady and placed on her bosom, and she then adorned them with precious stones, and offered them to her Divine Son. The Saint understood that those flowers were the afflictions which these Daughters of Mary and Spouses of Jesus had endured with Christian resignation, during the course of the Novena, preceding the festival.

Another time, whilst St. Gertrude was reciting the *Ave Maria* in choir with her religious Sisters, she saw three streams come forth from the Most Holy Trinity and meet together in the heart of the Blessed Virgin, descending from her and flowing over those who during these days recited this angelical salutation. It was on this occasion that she was taught to salute Our Lady, at least once a day, in these words: *Illos tuos misericordes oculos ad nos converte*, and was promised that, if she per severed in this practice during her whole life, she would receive the greatest consolations at the hour of her death.

Prayer.—O Mary, sovereign of the universe! our joy, our support and our defence! interest yourself in my favour before God, and obtain that I may be one day called to enjoy the happiness of heaven! I beseech you, O ever immaculate Virgin; I know you to be omnipotent with your Divine Son, for the salvation of sinners, and for the consolation of the afflicted, and I also know that you have need of no other recommendation than that of our miseries, for you are by excellence the Mother of Mercy. Amen.

Aspiration.—O my tender Mother! help me to live always united to your Divine Son Jesus.

Practice.—Consecrate yourself generously to Mary, and renew this consecration every Saturday.

Act of Consecration of St. Francis de Sales to the Most Holy Virgin

In concluding these pious exercises of the Month of Mary let us, in the spirit of St. Francis de Sales, recite the following Act of Consecration, which he often repeated to the Queen of Heaven, and in which the beauty of his soul and the purity of his heart are well depicted.

I salute you, most sweet Virgin Mary, Mother of God; you are my Mother and my Mistress; and therefore, I entreat you to accept me as your son and your servant; I wish to have no other Mother than you. I beg you, then, my good, and gracious, and most sweet Mother, to deign to console me in all my troubles and tribulations, both spiritual and corporal.

Remember, most sweet Virgin Mary, that you are my Mother, and that I am your son. You all powerful, and I poor, weak and vile. Nevertheless, I beseech you, O sweetest Mother, to keep me and defend me in all my ways and in all my actions, for, alas! I am poor and wretched, and in need of your most holy protection. Do, then, my beloved Mother, preserve and deliver my soul and body from all dangers and evils, and make me share in your blessings, your virtues, and, in particular, in your holy humility, your surpassing purity and your ardent charity.

Tell me not, gracious Virgin, that you cannot do so, because your Son gave you all power in heaven and on earth. Neither tell me that you ought not to hear me, for you are the common Mother of all poor mortals, and of me in particular. If you could not grant my prayer, then I should excuse you, saying: It is true that she is my Mother, and that I am her son, but she is not able to help me. If you were not my Mother, then, indeed, I should have patience, saying: She is rich enough to be able to assist me, but, alas! not being my Mother, she does not love me. But since, most sweet Virgin, you are not only my Mother, but are also powerful, how can you be excused if you do not console me, and come to my relief and assistance?

You see, my Mother, that it is difficult for you to reject any request that I may make you.

Be, then, exalted in heaven and on earth, glorious Virgin and dear Mother Mary, and, for the honour and glory of your Divine Son Jesus, accept me for your son, without regard to my miseries and sins. Deliver me from all evil of soul and body, obtain for me every virtue, and first of all humility; and bestow upon me all the benefits and graces necessary to make me pleasing to the Most Holy Trinity, Father, Son, and Holy Ghost. Amen.

THE END.